PRAISE FOR *THE*

"Quietly subversive, beautifuund,
Oliver Burkeman's book wil
—Alex Bellos, author of *Here's Looking at Euclid*

"What unites [Burkeman's] travels, and seems to drive the various
characters he meets, from modern-day Stoics to business consultants, is disillusionment with a patently false idea that something
as complex as the goal of human happiness can be found by
looking in a book . . . It's a simple idea, but an exhilarating and
satisfying one."
—Alexander Larman, *The Observer* (London)

"This is an excellent book; Burkeman makes us see that our current
approach, in which we want happiness but search for certainty—
often in the shape of material goods—is counterproductive."
—William Leith, *The Telegraph*

"Fascinating . . . After years spent consulting specialists—from
psychologists to philosophers and even Buddhists—Burkeman
realised they all agreed on one thing: . . . in order to be truly happy,
we might actually need to be willing to experience more negative
emotions—or, at least, to learn to stop running so hard from
them."
—Mandy Francis, *Daily Mail*

"Splendid . . . Readable and engaging."
—British chief rabbi Jonathan Sacks, *The Times* (London)

Nina Subin

Oliver Burkeman

The Antidote

Oliver Burkeman is the author of the *New York Times* bestseller *Four Thousand Weeks: Time Management for Mortals* and for many years wrote a popular column on psychology for *The Guardian*, "This Column Will Change Your Life." His work has appeared in *The New York Times*, *The Wall Street Journal*, *Psychologies*, and *New Philosopher*.

Also by Oliver Burkeman

Four Thousand Weeks: Time Management for Mortals

*Help! How to Become Slightly Happier and
Get a Bit More Done*

The Antidote

The Antidote

Happiness for People Who
Can't Stand Positive Thinking

Oliver Burkeman

Picador   Farrar, Straus and Giroux
New York

Picador
120 Broadway, New York 10271

Copyright © 2012 by Oliver Burkeman
All rights reserved
Printed in the United States of America
Originally published in 2012 by Canongate Books, Great Britain
Published in the United States in 2012 by Faber and Faber / Farrar,
Straus and Giroux
First paperback edition, 2013
Picador reissue edition, 2022

The Library of Congress has cataloged the Faber and Faber
hardcover edition as follows:
Burkeman, Oliver.
    The antidote : happiness for people who can't stand positive
thinking / Oliver Burkeman.
        p.   cm.
    Includes bibliographical references and index.
    ISBN 978-0-86547-941-8 (hbk. : alk. paper)
    1. Happiness.   2. Positive psychology.   3. Negativism.   I. Title.

BF575.H27 B86 2012
158—dc23

                                        2012022880

Paperback ISBN: 978-1-250-86040-8

Our books may be purchased in bulk for promotional, educational, or
business use. Please contact your local bookseller or the Macmillan
Corporate and Premium Sales Department at 1-800-221-7945,
extension 5442, or by email at MacmillanSpecialMarkets@macmillan.com.

Picador® is a U.S. registered trademark and is used by Macmillan Publishing
Group, LLC, under license from Pan Books Limited.

For book club information, please visit facebook.com/picadorbookclub or
email marketing@picadorusa.com.

picadorusa.com • instagram.com/picador
twitter.com/picadorusa • facebook.com/picadorusa

10   9   8   7   6   5

To my parents

I have always been fascinated by the law of reversed effort. Sometimes I call it 'the backwards law'. When you try to stay on the surface of the water, you sink; but when you try to sink, you float . . . Insecurity is the result of trying to be secure . . . contrariwise, salvation and sanity consist in the most radical recognition that we have no way of saving ourselves.   – Alan Watts, *The Wisdom of Insecurity*

I was going to buy a copy of *The Power of Positive Thinking*, and then I thought, 'What the hell good would that do?'
                                        – Ronnie Shakes

Contents

The Antidote

1

On Trying Too Hard to Be Happy

Try to pose for yourself this task: not to think of a polar bear, and you will see that the cursed thing will come to mind every minute.

– Fyodor Dostoevsky,
Winter Notes on Summer Impressions

THE MAN WHO CLAIMS that he is about to tell me the secret of human happiness is eighty-three years old, with an alarming orange tan that does nothing to enhance his credibility. It is just after eight o'clock on a December morning, in a darkened basketball stadium on the outskirts of San Antonio in Texas, and – according to the orange man – I am about to learn 'the one thing that will change your life forever'. I'm sceptical, but not as much as I might normally be, because I am only one of more than fifteen thousand people at Get Motivated!, America's 'most popular business motivational seminar', and the enthusiasm of my fellow audience members is starting to become infectious.

'So you wanna know?', asks the octogenarian, who is Dr Robert H. Schuller, veteran self-help guru, author of more than thirty-five books on the power of positive thinking, and, in his other job, the founding pastor of the largest church in the United States constructed entirely out of glass. The crowd roars its assent. Easily embarrassed British people like me do not, generally speaking, roar our assent at motivational seminars in Texas basketball stadiums, but the atmosphere partially overpowers my reticence. I roar quietly.

'Here it is, then,' Dr Schuller declares, stiffly pacing the stage, which is decorated with two enormous banners reading 'MOTIVATE!' and 'SUCCEED!', seventeen American flags, and a large number of potted plants. 'Here's the thing that will change your life forever.' Then he barks a single syllable – '*Cut!*' – and leaves a dramatic pause before completing his sentence: '. . . the word "impossible" out of your life! Cut it out! Cut it out forever!'

The audience combusts. I can't help feeling underwhelmed, but then I probably shouldn't have expected anything different from Get Motivated!, an event at which the sheer power of positivity counts for everything. 'You are the master of your destiny!' Schuller goes on. 'Think big, and dream bigger! Resurrect your abandoned hope! . . . Positive thinking works in *every area of life!*'

The logic of Schuller's philosophy, which is the doctrine of positive thinking at its most distilled, isn't exactly complex: decide to think happy and successful thoughts – banish the spectres of sadness and failure – and happiness and success will follow. It could be argued that not every speaker listed in the glossy brochure for today's seminar provides uncontroversial evidence in support of this outlook: the keynote speech is to be delivered, in a few hours' time, by George W. Bush, a president far from universally viewed as successful. But if you voiced this objection to Dr Schuller, he would probably dismiss it as 'negativity thinking'. To criticise the power of positivity is to demonstrate that you haven't really grasped it at all. If you had, you would stop grumbling about such things, and indeed about anything else.

The organisers of Get Motivated! describe it as a motivational seminar, but that phrase – with its suggestion of minor-league life coaches giving speeches in dingy hotel ballrooms – hardly captures the scale and grandiosity of the thing. Staged roughly once a month, in cities across North America, it sits at the summit of the global industry of positive thinking, and boasts an impressive roster of celebrity speakers: Mikhail Gorbachev and Rudy Giuliani are among the regulars, as are General Colin Powell and, somewhat incongruously, William Shatner. Should it ever occur to you that a formerly prominent figure in world politics (or William Shatner) has been keeping an inexplicably low profile in recent months, there's a good chance you'll find him or her at Get Motivated!, preaching the gospel of optimism.

As befits such celebrity, there's nothing dingy about the staging, either, which features banks of swooping spotlights, sound systems pumping out rock anthems, and expensive pyrotechnics; each speaker is welcomed to the stage amid showers of sparks and puffs of smoke. These special effects help propel the audience to ever higher altitudes of excitement, though it also doesn't hurt that for many of them, a trip to Get Motivated! means an extra day off work: many employers classify it as job training. Even the United States military, where 'training' usually means something more rigorous, endorses this view; in San Antonio, scores of the stadium's seats are occupied by uniformed soldiers from the local Army base.

Technically, I am here undercover. Tamara Lowe, the self-described 'world's number one female motivational speaker', who along with her husband runs the company behind Get Motivated!, has been accused of denying access to reporters, a tribe notoriously prone to negativity thinking. Lowe denies the charge, but out of caution, I've been describing myself as a 'self-employed

businessman' – a tactic, I'm realising too late, that only makes
me sound shifty. I needn't have bothered with subterfuge anyway,
it turns out, since I'm much too far away from the stage for the
security staff to be able to see me scribbling in my notebook. My
seat is described on my ticket as 'premier seating', but this turns
out to be another case of positivity run amok: at Get Motivated!,
there is only 'premier seating', 'executive seating', and 'VIP seating'.
In reality, mine is up in the nosebleed section; it is a hard plastic
perch, painful on the buttocks. But I am grateful for it, because
it means that by chance I'm seated next to a man who, as far as
I can make out, is one of the few cynics in the arena – an amiable,
large-limbed park ranger named Jim, who sporadically leaps to
his feet to shout 'I'm *so* motivated!' in tones laden with sarcasm.
He explains that he was required to attend by his employer, the
United States National Park Service, though when I ask why that
organisation might wish its rangers to use paid work time in this
fashion, he cheerily concedes that he has 'no fucking clue'.

Dr Schuller's sermon, meanwhile, is gathering pace. 'When I
was a child, it was impossible for a man ever to walk on the moon,
impossible to cut out a human heart and put it in another man's
chest . . . the word "impossible" has proven to be a very stupid
word!' He does not spend much time marshalling further evidence
for his assertion that failure is optional: it's clear that Schuller,
the author of *Move Ahead with Possibility Thinking* and *Tough
Times Never Last, but Tough People Do!*, vastly prefers inspiration
to argument. But in any case, he is really only a warm-up man
for the day's main speakers, and within fifteen minutes he is
striding away, to adulation and fireworks, fists clenched victori-
ously up at the audience, the picture of positive-thinking success.

It is only months later, back at my home in New York, reading
the headlines over morning coffee, that I learn the news that the

largest church in the United States constructed entirely from glass has filed for bankruptcy, a word Dr Schuller had apparently neglected to eliminate from his vocabulary.

For a civilisation so fixated on achieving happiness, we seem remarkably incompetent at the task. One of the best-known general findings of the 'science of happiness' has been the discovery that the countless advantages of modern life have done so little to lift our collective mood. The awkward truth seems to be that increased economic growth does not necessarily make for happier societies, just as increased personal income, above a certain basic level, doesn't make for happier people. Nor does better education, at least according to some studies. Nor does an increased choice of consumer products. Nor do bigger and fancier homes, which instead seem mainly to provide the privilege of more space in which to feel gloomy.

Perhaps you don't need telling that self-help books, the modern-day apotheosis of the quest for happiness, are among the things that fail to make us happy. But, for the record, research strongly suggests that they rarely much help. This is why, among themselves, some self-help publishers refer to the 'eighteen-month rule', which states that the person most likely to purchase any given self-help book is someone who, within the previous eighteen months, purchased a self-help book – one that evidently didn't solve all their problems. When you look at the self-help shelves with a coldly impartial eye, this isn't especially surprising. That we yearn for neat, book-sized solutions to the problem of being human is understandable, but strip away the packaging, and you'll find that the messages of such works are frequently banal. *The Seven Habits of Highly Effective People* essentially tells you to decide what matters most to you in life, and then do it; *How to Win Friends and Influence People* advises its readers to be pleasant rather than obnoxious, and to use people's first names a lot. One of the most successful management manuals of the last few years, *Fish!*, which is intended to help foster happiness and productivity in the workplace, suggests handing out small toy fish to your hardest-working employees.

As we'll see, when the messages get more specific than that, self-help gurus tend to make claims that simply aren't supported by more reputable research. The evidence suggests, for example, that venting your anger doesn't get rid of it, while visualising your goals doesn't seem to make you more likely to achieve them. And whatever you make of the country-by-country surveys of national happiness that are now published with some regularity, it's striking that the 'happiest' countries are never those where self-help books sell the most, nor indeed where professional psychotherapists are most widely consulted. The existence of a thriving 'happiness industry' clearly isn't sufficient to engender national happiness, and it's not unreasonable to suspect that it might make matters worse.

Yet the ineffectiveness of modern strategies for happiness is really just a small part of the problem. There are good reasons to believe that the whole notion of 'seeking happiness' is flawed to begin with. For one thing, who says happiness is a valid goal in the first place? Religions have never placed much explicit emphasis on it, at least as far as this world is concerned; philosophers have certainly not been unanimous in endorsing it, either. And any evolutionary psychologist will tell you that evolution has little interest in your being happy, beyond trying to make sure that you're not so listless or miserable that you lose the will to reproduce.

Even assuming happiness to be a worthy target, though, a worse

pitfall awaits, which is that aiming for it seems to reduce your
chances of ever attaining it. 'Ask yourself whether you are happy,'
observed the philosopher John Stuart Mill, 'and you cease to be
so.' At best, it would appear, happiness can only be glimpsed out
of the corner of an eye, not stared at directly. (We tend to
remember having been happy in the past much more frequently
than we are conscious of being happy in the present.) Making
matters worse still, what happiness actually *is* feels impossible to
define in words; even supposing you could do so, you'd presumably end up with as many different definitions as there are people
on the planet. All of which means it's tempting to conclude that
'How can we be happy?' is simply the wrong question – that we
might as well resign ourselves to never finding the answer, and
get on with something more productive instead.

But could there be a third possibility, besides the futile effort to
pursue solutions that never seem to work, on the one hand, and
just giving up, on the other? After several years reporting on the
field of psychology as a journalist, I finally realised that there
might be. I began to think that something united all those psychologists and philosophers – and even the occasional self-help guru
– whose ideas seemed actually to hold water. The startling conclusion at which they had all arrived, in different ways, was this: that
the effort to try to feel happy is often precisely the thing that makes
us miserable. And that it is our constant efforts to eliminate the
negative – insecurity, uncertainty, failure, or sadness – that is what
causes us to feel so insecure, anxious, uncertain, or unhappy. They
didn't see this conclusion as depressing, though. Instead, they
argued that it pointed to an alternative approach, a 'negative path'
to happiness, that entailed taking a radically different stance towards
those things that most of us spend our lives trying hard to avoid.
It involved learning to enjoy uncertainty, embracing insecurity,

stopping trying to think positively, becoming familiar with failure, even learning to value death. In short, all these people seemed to agree that in order to be truly happy, we might actually need to be willing to experience more negative emotions – or, at the very least, to learn to stop running quite so hard from them. Which is a bewildering thought, and one that calls into question not just our methods for achieving happiness, but also our assumptions about what 'happiness' really means.

These days, this notion certainly gets less press than the admonition to remain positive at all times. But it is a viewpoint with a surprisingly long and respectable history. You'll find it in the works of the Stoic philosophers of ancient Greece and Rome, who emphasised the benefits of always contemplating how badly things might go. It lies deep near the core of Buddhism, which counsels that true security lies in the unrestrained embrace of insecurity – in the recognition that we never really stand on solid ground, and never can. It underpins the medieval tradition of *memento mori*, which celebrated the life-giving benefits of never forgetting about death. And it is what connects New Age writers, such as the bestselling spiritual teacher Eckhart Tolle, with more mainstream recent work in cognitive psychology on the self-defeating nature of positive thinking. This same 'negative' approach to happiness also helps explain why so many people find mindfulness meditation so beneficial; why a new generation of business thinkers are advising companies to drop their obsession with goalsetting and embrace uncertainty instead; and why, in recent years, some psychologists have reached the conclusion that pessimism may often be as healthy and productive as optimism.

At the bottom of all this lies the principle that the countercultural philosopher of the 1950s and '60s, Alan Watts, echoing Aldous Huxley, labelled 'the law of reversed effort', or the 'backwards law':

the notion that in all sorts of contexts, from our personal lives to politics, all this *trying to make everything right* is a big part of what's wrong. Or, to quote Watts, that 'when you try to stay on the surface of the water, you sink; but when you try to sink, you float' and that 'insecurity is the result of trying to be secure'. In many cases, wrote Huxley, 'the harder we try with the conscious will to do something, the less we shall succeed'.

The negative path to happiness is not an argument for bloody-minded contrarianism at all costs: you won't do yourself any favours by walking into the path of oncoming buses, say, rather than trying to avoid them. Nor should it be taken as implying that there's necessarily anything wrong with optimism. A more useful way to think of it is as a much-needed counterweight to a culture fixated on the notion that optimism and positivity are the only possible paths to happiness. Of course, many of us are already healthily sceptical when it comes to positive thinking. But it is worth noting that even most people who disdain the 'cult of optimism', as the philosopher Peter Vernezze calls it, end up subtly endorsing it. They assume that since they cannot or will not subscribe to its ideology, their only alternative is to resign them-selves to gloom, or a sort of ironic curmudgeonhood, instead. The 'negative path' is about rejecting this dichotomy, and seeking instead the happiness that arises *through* negativity, rather than trying to drown negativity out with relentless good cheer. If a fixation on positivity is the disease, this approach is the antidote.

This 'negative path', it should be emphasised, isn't one single, comprehensive, neatly packaged philosophy; the antidote is not a panacea. Part of the problem with positive thinking, and many related approaches to happiness, is exactly this desire to reduce big questions to one-size-fits-all self-help tricks or ten-point plans. By contrast, the negative path offers no such single solution. Some of its proponents stress embracing negative feelings and thoughts, while others might better be described as advocating indifference towards them. Some focus on radically unconventional techniques for pursuing happiness, while others point towards a different definition of happiness, or to abandoning the pursuit of it altogether. The word 'negative' often has a double meaning here, too. It can refer to unpleasant experiences and emotions; but some philosophies of happiness are best described as 'negative' because they involve developing skills of 'not doing' – of learning not to chase positive feelings so aggressively. There are many paradoxes here, and they only get deeper the more you probe. For example, is a feeling or a situation truly 'negative' if it leads ultimately to happiness? If 'being positive' doesn't make you happy, is it right to call it 'being positive' at all? If you redefine happiness to accommodate negativity, is it still happiness? And so on. None of these questions can be tidily resolved. This is partly because the proponents of the negative path share only a general way of seeing life, rather than a single strict set of beliefs. But it is also because one crucial foundation of their approach is precisely that happiness involves paradoxes; that there is no way to tie up all the loose ends, however desperately we might want to.

This book is the record of a journey through the world of the 'backwards law', and of the people, living and dead, who have followed the negative path to happiness. My travels took me to the remote woodlands of Massachusetts, where I spent a week on a silent meditation retreat; to Mexico, where death is not shunned but celebrated; and to the desperately impoverished slums outside Nairobi, where insecurity is the unignorable reality of everyday life. I met modern-day Stoics, specialists in the art of failure, professional pessimists, and other advocates of the power of negative thinking, many of whom proved surprisingly jolly. But I began in San Antonio because I wanted to experience the cult of optimism at its most extreme. If it was true, as I had come to believe, that Dr Robert Schuller's flavour of positive thinking was really only an exaggerated version of the one-sided beliefs we all tend to hold about happiness, then it made sense, first of all, to witness the problem at its purest.

Which is how I came to find myself rising reluctantly to my feet, up in a dark extremity of that basketball stadium, because Get Motivated!'s excitable mistress of ceremonies had announced a 'dance competition', in which everyone present was obliged to participate. Giant beach balls appeared as if from nowhere, bumping across the heads of the crowd, who jiggled awkwardly as Wham! blared from the sound system. The first prize of a free trip to Disney World, we were informed, awaited not the best dancer but the *most motivated* one, though the distinction made little difference to me: I found the whole thing too excruciating to do more than sway very slightly. The prize was eventually awarded to a soldier. This was a decision that I suspected had been taken to pander to local patriotic pride, rather than strictly in recognition of highly motivated dancing.

After the competition, during a break in proceedings prior to George Bush's arrival, I left the main stadium to buy an overpriced hot dog, and found myself in conversation with a fellow attendee, an elegantly dressed retired schoolteacher from San Antonio who introduced herself as Helen. Money was tight, she explained when I asked why she was attending. She had reluctantly concluded that she needed to come out of retirement and get back to work, and she'd been hoping that Get Motivated! might motivate her.

'The thing is, though,' she said, as we chatted about the speakers we'd seen, 'it's kinda hard to think these good thoughts all the time like they tell you, isn't it?' For a moment, she looked stricken.

Then she recovered, wagging a teacherly finger as if to tell herself off. 'But you're not supposed to think like that!'

One of the foremost investigators of the problems with positive thinking was a professor of psychology named Daniel Wegner, who ran the Mental Control Laboratory at Harvard University. This is not, whatever its name might suggest, a CIA-funded establishment dedicated to the science of brainwashing. Wegner's intellectual territory was what has come to be known as 'ironic process theory', which explores the ways in which our efforts to suppress certain thoughts or behaviours result, ironically, in their becoming more prevalent. I got off to a bad start with Professor Wegner when I accidentally typed his surname, in a newspaper column, as 'Wenger'. He sent me a crabby email ('Get the name right!'), and didn't seem likely to be receptive to the argument that my slip-up was an interesting example of exactly the kinds of errors he studied. The rest of our communications proved a little strained.

The problems to which Wegner dedicated much of his career all have their origins in a simple and intensely irritating parlour game, which dates back at least to the days of Fyodor Dostoevsky, who reputedly used it to torment his brother. It takes the form of a challenge: can you – the victim is asked – succeed in *not* thinking about a white bear for one whole minute? You can guess the answer, of course, but it's nonetheless instructive to make the attempt. Why not try it now? Look at your watch, or find a clock with a second hand, and aim for a mere ten seconds of entirely non-white-bear-related thoughts, starting . . . now.

My commiserations on your failure.

Wegner's earliest investigations of ironic process theory

involved little more than issuing this challenge to American university students, then asking them to speak their inner monologues aloud while they made the attempt. This is a rather crude way of accessing someone's thought processes, but an excerpt from one typical transcript nonetheless vividly demonstrates the futility of the struggle:

> Of course, now the only thing I'm going to think about is a white bear . . . Don't think about a white bear. Ummm, what was I thinking about before? See, I think about flowers a lot . . . Okay, so my fingernails are really bad . . . Every time I really want, like . . . ummm . . . to talk, think, to not think about the white bear, then it makes me think about the white bear more . . .

At this juncture, you might be beginning to wonder why it is that some social psychologists seem to be allowed to spend other people's money proving the obvious. Of *course* the white bear challenge is virtually impossible to win. But Wegner was just getting started. The more he explored the field, the more he came to suspect that the internal mechanism responsible for sabotaging our efforts at suppressing white bear thoughts might govern an entire territory of mental activity and outward behaviour. The white bear challenge, after all, seems like a metaphor for much of what goes wrong in life: all too often, the outcome we're seeking to avoid is exactly the one to which we seem magnetically lured. Wegner labelled this effect 'the precisely counterintuitive error', which, he explained in one paper, 'is when we manage to do the worst possible thing, the blunder so outrageous that we think about it in advance and resolve not to let that happen. We see a rut coming up in the road ahead, and proceed to steer our bike

right into it. We make a mental note not to mention a sore point
in conversation, and then cringe in horror as we blurt out exactly
that thing. We carefully cradle the glass across the room, all the
while thinking "Don't spill", and then juggle it onto the carpet
under the gaze of our host.'

Far from representing an occasional divergence from our
otherwise flawless self-control, the capacity for ironic error seems
to lurk deep in the soul, close to the core of our characters. Edgar
Allan Poe, in his short story of the same name, calls it 'the imp
of the perverse': that nameless but distinct urge one sometimes
experiences, when walking along a precipitous cliff edge, or
climbing to the observation deck of a tall building, to throw
oneself off – not from any suicidal motivation, but precisely
because it would be so calamitous to do so. The imp of the
perverse plagues social interactions, too, as anyone who has ever
laughed in recognition at an episode of *Curb Your Enthusiasm*
will know all too well.

What is going on here, Wegner argues, is a malfunctioning
of the uniquely human capacity for metacognition, or thinking
about thinking. 'Metacognition', Wegner explains, 'occurs when
thought takes itself as an object.' Mainly, it's an extremely useful
skill: it is what enables us to recognise when we are being unreasonable, or sliding into depression, or being afflicted by anxiety,
and then to do something about it. But when we use metacognitive thoughts directly to try to control our other, everyday, 'object-
level' thoughts – by suppressing images of white bears, say, or
replacing gloomy thoughts with happy ones – we run into trouble.
'Metathoughts are instructions we give ourselves about our
object-level thinking,' as Wegner puts it, 'and sometimes we just
can't follow our own instructions.'

When you try not to think of a white bear, you may experience some success in forcing alternative thoughts into your mind. At the same time, though, a metacognitive monitoring process will crank into action, to scan your mind for evidence of whether you are succeeding or failing at the task. And this is where things get perilous, because if you try too hard – or, Wegner's studies suggest, if you are tired, stressed, depressed, attempting to multi-task, or otherwise suffering from 'mental load' – metacognition will frequently go wrong. The monitoring process will start to occupy more than its fair share of limelight on the cognitive stage. It will jump to the forefront of consciousness – and suddenly, all you will be able to think about is white bears, and how badly you're doing at not thinking about them.

Could it be that ironic process theory also sheds light on what is wrong with our efforts to achieve happiness, and on the way that our efforts to feel positive seem so frequently to bring about the opposite result? In the years since Wegner's earliest white bear experiments, his research, and that of others, has turned up more and more evidence to support that notion. One example: when experimental subjects are told of an unhappy event, but then instructed to try *not* to feel sad about it, they end up feeling worse than people who are informed of the event, but given no instructions about how to feel. In another study, when patients who were suffering from panic disorders listened to relaxation tapes, their hearts beat faster than patients who listened to audiobooks with no explicitly 'relaxing' content. Bereaved people who make the most effort to avoid feeling grief, research suggests, take the longest to recover from their loss. Our efforts at mental suppression fail in the sexual arena, too: people instructed not to think about sex exhibit greater arousal, as measured by the electrical conductivity of their skin, than those not instructed to suppress such thoughts.

Seen from this perspective, swathes of the self-help industry's favourite techniques for achieving happiness and success – from positive thinking to visualising your goals to 'getting motivated' – stand revealed to be suffering from one enormous flaw. A person who has resolved to 'think positive' must constantly scan his or her mind for negative thoughts – there's no other way that the mind could ever gauge its success at the operation – yet that scanning will draw attention to the presence of negative thoughts. (Worse, if the negative thoughts start to predominate, a vicious spiral may kick in, since the failure to think positively may become the trigger for a new stream of self-berating thoughts, about not thinking positively enough.) Suppose you decide to follow Dr Schuller's suggestion and try to eliminate the word 'impossible' from your vocabulary, or more generally try to focus exclusively on successful outcomes, and stop thinking about things not working out. As we'll see, there are all sorts of problems with this approach. But the most basic one is that you may well fail, as a result of the very act of monitoring your success.

This problem of self-sabotage through self-monitoring is not the only hazard of positive thinking. An additional twist was revealed in 2009, when a psychologist based in Canada named Joanne Wood set out to test the effectiveness of 'affirmations', those peppy self-congratulatory phrases designed to lift the user's mood through repetition. Affirmations have their origins in the work of the nineteenth-century French pharmacist Émile Coué, a forerunner of the contemporary positive thinkers, who coined the one that remains the most famous: 'Every day, in every way, I am getting better and better.'

Most affirmations sound pretty cheesy, and one might suspect that they would have little effect. Surely, though, they're harmless? Wood wasn't so sure about that. Her reasoning, though compatible with Wegner's, drew on a different psychological tradition known as 'self-comparison theory'. Much as we like to hear positive messages about ourselves, this theory suggests, we crave even more strongly the sense of being a coherent, consistent self in the first place. Messages that conflict with that existing sense of self, therefore, are unsettling, and so we often reject them – even if they happen to be positive, and even if the source of the message is ourselves. Wood's hunch was that people who seek out affirmations would be, by definition, those with low self-esteem – but that, for that very same reason, they would end up reacting against the messages in the affirmations, because they conflicted with their self-images. Messages such as 'Every day, in every way, I am getting better and better' would clash with their poor opinion of themselves, and thus be rejected, so as not to threaten the coherence of their sense of self. The result might even be a worsening of their low self-esteem as people struggled to reassert their existing self-images against the incoming messages.

Which is exactly what happened in Wood's research. In one set of experiments, people were divided into subgroups of those with low and high self-esteem, then asked to undertake a journal-writing exercise; every time a bell rang, they were to repeat to themselves the phrase 'I am a lovable person.' According to a variety of ingenious mood measures, those who began the process with low self-esteem became appreciably less happy as a result of telling themselves that they were lovable. They didn't feel particularly lovable to begin with – and trying to convince themselves otherwise merely solidified their negativity. 'Positive thinking' had made them feel worse.

The arrival of George Bush onstage in San Antonio was heralded by the sudden appearance of his Secret Service detail. These were men who would probably have stood out anywhere, in their dark suits and earpieces, but who stood out twice as prominently at Get Motivated! thanks to their rigid frowns. The job of protecting former presidents from potential assassins, it appeared, wasn't one that rewarded looking on the bright side and assuming that nothing could go wrong.

Bush himself, by contrast, bounded onstage grinning. 'You know, retirement ain't so bad, especially when you get to retire to Texas!' he began, before launching into a speech he had evidently delivered several times before. First, he told a folksy anecdote about spending his post-presidency cleaning up after his dog ('I was picking up that which I had been dodging for eight years!'). Then, for a strange moment or two, it seemed as if the main topic of his speech would be how he once had to choose a rug for the Oval Office ('I thought to myself, the presidency is going to be a decision-making experience!'). But his real subject, it soon emerged, was optimism. 'I don't believe you can lead a family, or a school, or a city, or a state, or a country, unless you're optimistic that the future is going to be better,' he said. 'And I want you to know that, even in the darkest days of my presidency, I was optimistic that the future was going to be better than the past for our citizens and the world.'

You need not hold any specific political opinion about the forty-third president of the United States to see how his words illustrate a fundamental strangeness of the 'cult of optimism'. Bush was not ignoring the numerous controversies of his administration – the strategy one might have imagined he would adopt at a motivational seminar, before a sympathetic audience and facing no risk of hostile questions. Instead, he had chosen to redefine them as evidence in support of his optimistic attitude. The way Bush saw it, the happy and successful periods of his presidency proved the benefits of an optimistic outlook, of course – but so did the unhappy and unsuccessful ones. When things are going badly, after all, you need optimism all the more. Or to put it another way: once you have resolved to embrace the ideology of positive thinking, you will find a way to interpret virtually any eventuality as a justification for thinking positively. You need never spend time considering how your actions might go wrong.

Could this curiously unfalsifiable ideology of positivity at all costs – positivity regardless of the results – be actively dangerous? Opponents of the Bush administration's foreign policies might have reason to think so. This is also one part of the case made by the social critic Barbara Ehrenreich, in her 2009 book *Bright-Sided: How Positive Thinking Is Undermining America*. One underappreciated cause of the global financial crisis of the late 2000s, she argues, was an American business culture in which even thinking about the possibility of failure – let alone speaking up about it at meetings – had come to be considered an embarrassing *faux pas*. Bankers, their narcissism stoked by a culture that awarded grand ambition above all, lost the capacity to distinguish between their ego-fuelled dreams and concrete results. Meanwhile, homebuyers assumed that whatever they wanted could be theirs if they wanted it badly enough (how many of them had read books such as *The Secret*, which makes exactly that claim?) and accordingly sought mortgages they were unable to repay. Irrational optimism suffused the financial sector, and the professional purveyors of optimism – the speakers and self-help gurus and seminar organisers – were only too happy to encourage it. 'To the extent that positive thinking had become a business in itself,' writes Ehrenreich, 'business was its principal client, eagerly consuming the good news that all things are possible through an effort of mind. This was a useful message for employees, who by the turn of the twenty-first

century were being required to work longer hours for fewer benefits
and diminishing job security. But it was also a liberating ideology
for top-level executives. What was the point in agonising over
balance sheets and tedious analyses of risks – and why bother
worrying about dizzying levels of debt and exposure to potential
defaults – when all good things come to those who are optimistic
enough to expect them?'

Ehrenreich traces the origins of this philosophy to nineteenth-
century America, and specifically to the quasi-religious movement
known as New Thought. New Thought arose in rebellion against
the dominant, gloomy message of American Calvinism, which was
that relentless hard work was the duty of every Christian – with
the additional sting that, thanks to the doctrine of predestination,
you might in any case already be marked to spend eternity in
Hell. New Thought, by contrast, proposed that one could achieve
happiness and worldly success through the power of the mind.
This mind-power could even cure physical ailments, according
to the newly minted religion of Christian Science, which grew
directly from the same roots. Yet, as Ehrenreich makes clear, New
Thought imposed its own kind of harsh judgmentalism, replacing
Calvinism's obligatory hard work with obligatory positive
thinking. Negative thoughts were fiercely denounced – a message
that echoed 'the old religion's condemnation of sin' and added
'an insistence on the constant interior labour of self-examination'.
Quoting the sociologist Micki McGee, Ehrenreich shows how,
under this new orthodoxy of optimism, 'continuous and never-
ending work on the self [was] offered not only as a road to success,
but also to a kind of secular salvation'.

George Bush, then, was standing in a venerable tradition when
he proclaimed the importance of optimism in all circumstances.
But his speech at Get Motivated! was over almost as soon as it had

started. A dash of religion, a singularly unilluminating anecdote about the terrorist attacks of 11 September 2001, some words of praise for the military, and he was waving goodbye – 'Thank you, Texas, it's good to be home!' – as his bodyguards closed in around him. Beneath the din of cheering, I heard Jim, the park ranger in the next seat, emit a sigh of relief. 'OK, I'm motivated now,' he muttered, to nobody in particular. 'Is it time for some beer?'

'There are lots of ways of being miserable,' says a character in a short story by Edith Wharton, 'but there's only one way of being comfortable, and that is to stop running around after happiness.' This observation pungently expresses the problem with the 'cult of optimism' – the ironic, self-defeating struggle that sabotages positivity when we try too hard. But it also hints at the possibility of a more hopeful alternative, an approach to happiness that might take a radically different form. The first step is to learn how to stop chasing positivity so intently. But many of the proponents of the 'negative path' to happiness take things further still, arguing – paradoxically, but persuasively – that deliberately plunging more deeply into what we think of as negative may be a precondition of true happiness.

Perhaps the most vivid metaphor for this whole strange philosophy is a small children's toy known as the 'Chinese finger trap', though the evidence suggests it is probably not Chinese in origin at all. In his office at the University of Nevada, the psychologist Steven Hayes, an outspoken critic of counterproductive positive thinking, keeps a box of them on his desk; he uses them to illustrate his arguments. The 'trap' is a tube, made of thin strips of woven bamboo, with the opening at each end being roughly the size of a human finger. The unwitting victim is asked to insert his index fingers into the tube, then finds himself trapped: in reaction to his efforts to pull his fingers out again, the openings at each end of the tube constrict, gripping his fingers ever more tightly. The harder he pulls, the more decisively he is trapped. It is only by relaxing his efforts at escape, and by pushing his fingers further in, that he can widen the ends of the tube, whereupon it falls away, and he is free.

In the case of the Chinese finger trap, Hayes observes, 'doing the presumably sensible thing is counterproductive'.

Following the negative path to happiness is about doing the other thing – the presumably illogical thing – instead.

2

What Would Seneca Do?

The Stoic Art of Confronting the Worst-Case Scenario

Pessimism, when you get used to it, is just as agreeable as optimism.

– Arnold Bennett, *Things That Have Interested Me*

IT IS AN ORDINARY spring morning on the Central Line of the London Underground, which is to say that there are the usual 'minor delays' to the service, and a major sense of despair emanating from the closely packed commuters. The only extraordinary thing is that I am a few moments from undergoing, entirely voluntarily, what I expect to be one of the most terrifying experiences of my life. As we approach Chancery Lane station – but before the automated voice on the public-address system announces this fact – I plan to break the silence and proclaim, loudly, the words 'Chancery Lane'. As the train continues to Holborn, Tottenham Court Road, Oxford Circus and beyond, it is my intention to keep this up, announcing the name of each station as we go.

I am aware that this is not the most frightening exploit imaginable. Readers with experience of having been taken hostage by pirates, or buried alive – or even just having endured a particularly turbulent aeroplane journey, for that matter – could be forgiven for finding this all rather self-dramatising. Yet the fact remains that my palms are sweating and my heartbeat is accelerating. I've never handled embarrassment well, and now I'm berating myself for ever having thought that deliberately courting it might be a clever idea.

I am conducting this ritual of deliberate self-humiliation on the instructions of a modern-day psychologist, Albert Ellis, who died in 2007. But he designed it to provide a vivid demonstration of an ancient philosophy, that of the Stoics, who were among the first to suggest that the path to happiness might depend on negativity. Ellis recommended the 'subway-station exercise', originally prescribed to his therapy patients in New York, as a way of demonstrating how irrationally we approach even mildly unpleasant experiences – and how we might find unforeseen benefits lurking within them, if only we could bring ourselves to look.

Stoicism, which was born in Greece and matured in Rome, should not be confused with 'stoicism' as the word is commonly used today – a weary, uncomplaining resignation that better describes the attitude of my fellow passengers on the Underground. Real Stoicism is far more tough-minded, and involves developing a kind of muscular calm in the face of trying circumstances. This is also the purpose of Ellis's excruciating exercise, which is intended to bring me face to face with all my unspoken beliefs about embarrassment, self-consciousness, and what other people might think about me. It will force me to experience the unpleasantness that I am fearing, and thereby to realise something about the situation that is psychologically intriguing: that my beliefs about how staggeringly awful it's going to be, when they're brought out into the open and examined, just don't seem to match the facts.

Unless you are an unusually unembarrassable person, you can

probably empathise with the apprehension I am feeling – yet when you think about it, there's something bizarre about having any negative feelings whatsoever in this situation. After all, I know nobody in the carriage personally, so I have nothing to lose from them thinking that I'm crazy. Moreover, I know from past experience on the Underground that when other people start talking out loud to themselves, I ignore them, as does everyone else; this is almost certainly the worst that's going to happen to me. And those other people speaking out loud are often talking gibberish, whereas I am going to be announcing the names of the stations. You could almost argue that I'm performing a public service. Certainly, it will be much less irritating than all the leaking iPod headphones in my vicinity.

And so why – as the train begins to slow, almost indetectibly at first, for the approach to Chancery Lane – do I feel as if I want to vomit?

Behind many of the most popular approaches to happiness is the simple philosophy of *focusing on things going right*. In the world of self-help, the most overt expression of this outlook is the technique known as 'positive visualisation': if you mentally picture things turning out well, the reasoning goes, they are far more likely to do so. The fashionable New Age concept of the 'law of attraction' takes things a step further, suggesting that visualisation may be the *only* thing you need in order to attain riches, great relationships, and good health. 'There is a deep tendency in human nature to become precisely what you visualise yourself as being,' said Norman Vincent Peale, the author of *The Power of Positive Thinking*, in a speech he gave to executives of the investment bank Merrill Lynch in the mid-1980s. 'If you see yourself as tense and nervous and frustrated . . . that, assuredly, is what you will be. If you see yourself as inferior in any way, and you hold that image in your conscious mind, it will presently, by the process of intellectual osmosis, sink into the unconscious, and you will be what you visualise. If, on the contrary, you see yourself as organised, controlled, studious, a thinker, a worker, believing in your talent and ability and yourself, that is what you will become.' Merrill Lynch collapsed in the financial meltdown of 2008 and had to be rescued by Bank of America; readers are invited to draw their own conclusions.

Even most people who scoff at Peale's homilies, however, might find it hard to argue with the underlying outlook: that being optimistic about the future, when you can manage it, is generally for the best. And focusing on how you hope things will turn out, rather than how you hope they won't, seems like a sensible way of motivating yourself and of maximising your chances of success. Walking into a job interview, you're surely better off to err on the side of assuming you can triumph. As you prepare to ask someone on a date, it's surely advisable to operate on the basis that she or he might actually say yes. Indeed, a tendency to look on the bright side may be so intertwined with human survival that evolution has skewed us that way. In her 2011 book *The Optimism Bias*, the neuroscientist Tali Sharot compiles growing evidence that a well-functioning mind may be built so as to perceive the odds of things going well as greater than they really are. Healthy and happy people, research suggests, generally have a *less* accurate, overly optimistic grasp of their true ability to influence events than do those who are suffering from depression.

Yet there are problems with this outlook, aside from just feeling disappointed when things don't turn out well. These are particularly acute in the case of positive visualisation. Over the last few years, the German-born psychologist Gabriele Oettingen and her colleagues have constructed a series of experiments designed to unearth the truth about 'positive fantasies about the future'. The results are striking: spending time and energy thinking about how well things could go, it has emerged, actually reduces most people's motivation to achieve them. Experimental subjects who were encouraged to think about how they were going to have a particularly high-achieving week at work, for example, ended up achieving less than those who were invited to reflect on the coming week, but given no further guidelines on how to do so.

In one ingenious experiment, Oettingen had some of the participants rendered mildly dehydrated. They were then taken through an exercise that involved visualising drinking a refreshing, icy glass of water, while others took part in a different exercise. The dehydrated water-visualisers – contrary to the self-help doctrine of motivation through visualisation – experienced a significant *reduction* in their energy levels, as measured by blood pressure. Far from becoming more motivated to hydrate themselves, their bodies relaxed, as if their thirst were already quenched. In experiment after experiment, people responded to positive visualisation by relaxing. They seemed, subconsciously, to have confused visualising success with having already achieved it.

It doesn't necessarily follow, of course, that it would be a better idea to switch to *negative* visualisation instead, and to start focusing on all the ways in which things could go wrong. Yet that is precisely one of the conclusions that emerges from Stoicism, a school of philosophy that originated in Athens, a few years after the death of Aristotle, and that came to dominate Western thinking about happiness for nearly five centuries.

The first Stoic, so far as we know, was Zeno of Citium, born in what is now Larnaca, on the southern shores of Cyprus, sometime around 334 BC. 'He had his head naturally bent on one side,' writes the third-century Greek historian Diogenes Laertius, in his *Lives and Opinions of Eminent Philosophers*, which is the primary source of evidence for the early Stoics. 'He was thin, very tall, of a dark complexion, [with] flabby, weak legs . . . and he was very fond, as it is said, of figs, both fresh and dried in the sun.' According to legend, Zeno was a merchant who came to Athens aged around thirty, possibly after the traumatising experience of being shipwrecked. There, he began to study under the Cynic philosopher Crates; Laertius relates one of Zeno's early experiences at the hands of Crates, which may help explain Stoicism's focus on irrational beliefs as the source of emotional distress. According to the story, Crates gave Zeno a bowl of 'lentil porridge' and demanded that he carry it through the streets of Athens, but then Crates smashed the bowl with his stick, causing the contents to splatter all over Zeno's body. 'The porridge ran all down his legs,' Laertius tells us, whereupon Zeno ran away in embarrassment. 'Why do you run away [when] you have done no harm?', Crates called after him teasingly, mocking Zeno's belief that he had grounds for feeling ashamed. When Zeno began to teach philosophy himself, he did so under the *stoa poikile*, the 'painted porch' on the north side of the ancient agora of Athens – hence the label 'Stoic'. The school's influence subsequently spread to Rome, and it is these later Roman Stoics – above all Epictetus, Seneca the Younger, and Marcus Aurelius – whose works have survived.

From their earliest days, Stoic teachings emphasised the fundamental importance of reason. Nature had bestowed uniquely upon humans, the Stoics argued, the capacity to reason, and therefore a 'virtuous' life – meaning a life proper and fitting to a human – entailed living in accordance with reason. The

Roman Stoics added a psychological twist: living virtuously in accordance with reason, they argued, would lead to inner tranquility – 'a state of mind', writes the scholar of Stoicism William Irvine, 'marked by the absence of negative emotions, such as grief, anger, and anxiety, and the presence of positive emotions, such as joy.' And here lies the essential difference between Stoicism and the modern-day 'cult of optimism'. For the Stoics, the ideal state of mind was tranquility, not the excitable cheer that positive thinkers usually seem to mean when they use the word 'happiness'. And tranquility was to be achieved not by strenuously chasing after enjoyable experiences, but by cultivating a kind of calm indifference towards one's circumstances. One way to do this, the Stoics argued, was by turning towards negative emotions and experiences; not shunning them, but examining them closely instead.

If this focus on negativity seems perverse, it may help to consider the life circumstances of the Stoics themselves. Epictetus was born into slavery in what is now Turkey; though later freed, he died crippled as a result of his masters' brutal treatment. Seneca, by contrast, was the son of a nobleman, and enjoyed a stellar career as a personal tutor to the Roman Emperor. But that ended abruptly when his employer – who, unfortunately, was the deranged Nero – suspected Seneca of plotting against him, and ordered him to commit suicide. There seems to have been little evidence for Nero's suspicions, but by that point he had already murdered his mother and step-brother, and gained a reputation for burning Christians in his gardens after dark to provide a source of light, so he can hardly be accused of acting out of character. Seneca, the story goes, tried to do as he was told, by cutting open his veins to bleed himself to death. But he failed to die, and so asked to be fed poison; this, too, failed to kill him. It was only when he took a suffocatingly steamy bath that he finally expired. Perhaps it is unsurprising that a philosophy emerging from such circumstances as Epictetus's – or in a context where a fate such as Seneca's awaited even those of noble birth, if their luck ran out – would not incline towards positive thinking. Where was the merit in trying to convince yourself that things would turn out for the best, when there was so much evidence that they might not?

Yet it is a curious truth that the Stoics' approach to happiness through negativity begins with exactly the kind of insight that Norman Vincent Peale might endorse: that when it comes to feeling upbeat or despondent, it's our *beliefs* that really matter. Most of us, the Stoics point out, go through life under the delusion that it is certain people, situations, or events that make us sad, anxious, or angry. When you're irritated by a colleague at the next desk who won't stop talking, you naturally assume that the colleague is the source of the irritation; when you hear that a beloved relative is ill and feel pained for them, it makes sense to think of the illness as the source of the pain. Look closely at your experience, though, say the Stoics, and you will eventually be forced to conclude that neither of these external events is 'negative' in itself. Indeed, nothing outside your own mind can properly be described as negative or positive at all. What actually causes suffering are the beliefs you hold about those things. The colleague is not irritating per se, but because of your belief that getting your work finished without interruption is an important goal. Even a relative's illness is bad only in view of your belief that it's a good thing for your relatives not to be ill. (Millions of people, after all, get ill every day; we have no beliefs whatsoever about most of them, and consequently don't feel distressed.) 'Things do not touch the soul,' is how Marcus Aurelius, the Stoic philosopher–emperor, expresses the notion, adding: 'Our perturbations come only from the opinion which is within.' We think of distress as a one-step procedure: something in the outside world causes distress in your interior world. In fact, it's a two-step procedure: between the outside event and the inside emotion is a belief. If you didn't judge a relative's illness to be bad, would you be distressed by it? Obviously not. 'There is nothing either good or bad, but thinking makes it so,' Shakespeare has Hamlet say, very Stoically indeed.

The suggestion here is not that negative emotions don't really exist, or that they don't matter, or that they can easily be brushed aside through sheer force of will. The Stoics aren't making any such claims; they are merely specifying the mechanism through which all distress arises. And they do mean all. Even losing your home or your job or a loved one, from this perspective, is not a negative event in itself; in itself, it's merely an event. To which you might respond: But what if it really *is* bad? Lacking a home and an income, you might perish from starvation or exposure. Surely that would be bad? But the same relentless logic applies. What makes the prospect of starvation or exposure distressing in the first place? The beliefs that you hold about the disadvantages of death. This view of how emotions work, as the leading Stoic scholar A. A. Long points out, is the underlying insight behind contemporary cognitive behavioural therapy, too. 'It's all there [in the work of the Stoics],' he told me. 'Particularly this idea that judgments are in our power, that our emotions are determined by our judgments, and that we can always step back and ask: "Is it other people that bother me? Or the judgment I make about other people?"' It was a method of thinking he regularly employed himself, Long explained, to deal with everyday distresses, such as road rage. Were other drivers really behaving 'badly'? Or was it more accurate to say that the cause of his anger was his belief that they ought to behave differently?

The distinction is crucial. The idea that it is ultimately our beliefs that cause our distress, as we've seen, is a perspective shared by Stoics and positive thinkers alike. Beyond this, though, the two traditions diverge utterly – and the divergence becomes most baldly apparent when it comes to beliefs about the future. The evangelists of optimism argue that you should cultivate as many positive expectations about the future as you can. But this is not the good idea that it may at first appear to be. For a start, as Gabriele Oettingen's experiments demonstrate, focusing on the outcome you desire may actually sabotage your efforts to achieve it. More generally, a Stoic would point out, it just isn't a particularly good technique for feeling happier. Ceaseless optimism about the future only makes for a greater shock when things go wrong; by fighting to maintain only positive beliefs about the future, the positive thinker ends up being *less* prepared, and *more* acutely distressed, when things eventually happen that he can't persuade himself to believe are good. (And such things will happen.) This is a problem underlying all approaches to happiness that set too great a store by optimism. Trying to see things in an exclusively positive light is an attitude that requires constant, effortful replenishment. Should your efforts falter or prove insufficient when confronted by some unexpected shock, you'll sink back down into – possibly deeper – gloom.

Applying their stringent rationality to the situation, the Stoics propose a more elegant, sustainable and calming way to deal with the possibility of things going wrong: rather than struggling to avoid all thought of these worst-case scenarios, they counsel actively dwelling on them, staring them in the face. Which brings us to an important milestone on the negative path to happiness – a psychological tactic that William Irvine argues is 'the single most valuable technique in the Stoics' toolkit'. He calls it 'negative visualisation'. The Stoics themselves, rather more pungently, called it 'the premeditation of evils'.

The first benefit of dwelling on how bad things might get is a straightforward one. Psychologists have long agreed that one of the greatest enemies of human happiness is 'hedonic adaptation' – the predictable and frustrating way in which any new source of pleasure we obtain, whether it's as minor as a new piece of electronic gadgetry or as major as a marriage, swiftly gets relegated to the backdrop of our lives. We grow accustomed to it, and so it ceases to deliver so much joy. It follows, then, that regularly reminding yourself that you might lose any of the things you currently enjoy – indeed, that you will definitely lose them all, in the end, when death catches up with you – would reverse the adaptation effect. Thinking about the possibility of losing something you value shifts it from the backdrop of your life back to centre stage, where it can deliver pleasure once more. 'Whenever you grow attached to something,' writes Epictetus, 'do not act as though it were one of those things that cannot be taken away, but as though it were something like a jar or a crystal goblet . . . if you kiss your child, your brother, your friend . . remind yourself that you love a mortal, something not your own; it has been given to you for the present, not inseparably nor forever, but like a fig, or a bunch of grapes, at a fixed season of the year.' Each time you kiss your child goodnight, he contends, you should specifically consider the possibility that she might die tomorrow. This is jarring advice that might strike any parent as horrifying, but Epictetus is adamant: the practice will make you love her all the more, while simultaneously reducing the shock should that awful eventuality ever come to pass.

The second, subtler, and arguably even more powerful benefit of the premeditation of evils is as an antidote to anxiety. Consider how we normally seek to assuage worries about the future: we seek reassurance, looking to persuade ourselves that everything will be all right. But reassurance is a double-edged sword. In the short term, it can be wonderful, but like all forms of optimism, it requires constant maintenance: if you offer reassurance to a friend who is in the grip of anxiety, you'll often find that a few days later, he'll be back for more. Worse, reassurance can actually exacerbate anxiety: when you reassure your friend that the worst-case scenario he fears probably won't occur, you inadvertently reinforce his belief that it would be catastrophic if it did. You are tightening the coil of his anxiety, not loosening it. All too often, the Stoics point out, things will not turn out for the best.

But it is also true that, when they do go wrong, they'll almost certainly go *less* wrong than you were fearing. Losing your job won't condemn you to starvation and death; losing a boyfriend or girl-friend won't condemn you to a life of unrelenting misery. Those fears are based on irrational judgments about the future, usually because you haven't thought the matter through in sufficient detail. You heard the rumour about cutbacks at the company, and instantly jumped to a mental image of being utterly destitute; a lover behaved coldly and you leapt to imagining lifelong loneliness. The premed-itation of evils is the way to replace these irrational notions with more rational judgments: spend time vividly imagining exactly how wrong things could go *in reality*, and you will usually find that your fears were exaggerated. If you lost your job, there are specific steps you could take to find a new one; if you lost your relation-ship, you would probably manage to find some happiness in life despite being single. Confronting the worst-case scenario saps it of much of its anxiety-inducing power. Happiness reached via positive thinking can be fleeting and brittle; negative visualisation generates a vastly more dependable calm.

Seneca pushes this way of thinking to its logical conclusion. If visualising the worst can be a source of tranquility, what about deliberately trying to experience a taste of the worst? In one of his letters, he proposes an exercise that was the direct predecessor of my adventures in embarrassment on the London Underground, though admittedly more extreme. If what you fear the most is losing your material wealth, he advises, don't try to persuade yourself that it could never happen. (That would be the Dr Robert H. Schuller approach: refusing to countenance the possibility of failure.) Instead, try acting as if you had already lost it. 'Set aside a certain number of days, during which you shall be content with the scantiest and cheapest fare, with coarse and rough dress,' he suggests, 'saying to yourself the while: "Is this the condition that I feared?".' You may not have much fun. But the exercise will force a collision between your wildest anxieties about how bad such an eventuality might be, on the one hand, and on the other, the reality – which may be unpleasant, but also much less catastrophic. It will help you grasp that the worst-case scenario is something with which you would be able to cope.

This all made intellectual sense to me, but I wanted to know if anyone really lived according to these principles today. I had heard rumours of a contemporary community of self-described Stoics, scattered around the globe, and my research brought me swiftly to something called the International Stoic Forum, an internet message-board with more than eight hundred members. Further investigation led to the story of a police officer in Chicago, who claimed to use the principles of Stoicism to keep calm while confronting violent gang members. At another website, a school-teacher from Florida reported back from the inaugural meeting of the International Stoic Society, held in Cyprus in 1998. Throughout all this, one name kept cropping up – as a moderator of the International Stoic Forum, as the tutor to the Chicago cop, and as the author of numerous web postings on the benefits of living Stoically. My intention had been to track down a Seneca for the modern era. I imagined that this person might have chosen to shun society, as Seneca did in his later years; that he might live, for example, in a simple rustic dwelling in the foothills of some Mediterranean volcano, spending his days in philosophical contemplation and his evenings drinking retsina. But the person to whom my enquiries led, in the event, was none of these things. His name was Keith, and he lived a short train ride to the north-west of central London, in the town of Watford.

Despite living in Watford, Dr Keith Seddon did fulfill certain criteria of otherworldliness. This became clear as soon as I saw his house. Set back from its better-kept neighbours by a tall hedgerow, in which I eventually located a very small gate, it resembled a wizard's cottage as conceived by Tolkien, had *The Lord of the Rings* been set in the London commuter belt. It was early afternoon, and raining hard. The front room, I gathered by peering through the large bay window, was empty of people, but crammed with teetering piles of books, along with an extensive collection of panama hats. It took several rings of the doorbell before Seddon answered. But when he did, he looked the part: a long grey beard, twinkling eyes, and a leather waistcoat, the whole thing topped off by one of his panamas. 'Come in,' he said, three times in a row, then led me out of the rain, through the hallway, and into a small side room containing a gas fire, a sofa, and two high-backed armchairs. In one of them sat his wife, Jocelyn. Much of the remaining space was taken up by still more books, squeezed into insufficient bookcases. Works of classical philosophy jostled against more esoteric titles: *The Book of Egyptian Ritual*, *An Introduction to Elvish*, and *Fountain Pens of the World*. Seddon ushered me to the sofa and went to fetch me a Diet Coke.

It was immediately evident that fate had not been especially kind to the couple. Jocelyn suffered from severe early-onset rheumatoid arthritis, which had left her badly debilitated. Though she was only in her early fifties, she now had great difficulty even raising a glass to her lips, a manoeuvre that required the use of both hands and clearly caused her pain. Keith was her full-time carer, and suffered himself from myalgic encephalomyelitis, or chronic fatigue syndrome. Both had PhDs and had planned on academic careers, but then Jocelyn's illness had got in the way. Now Keith's work as a tutor of correspondence courses in Stoicism, teaching students at private American universities, was drying up, too, and money was seriously tight.

Yet the atmosphere in the overheated little room was far from despondent. Jocelyn, it emerged, didn't describe herself as a Stoic like her husband, but shared a similar cast of mind: she said her illness had proven to be a 'dark gift', and that once she'd learned to ignore the people telling her to 'fight' it or to 'think positive', she had come to understand her dependence on others as a kind of blessing. She seemed serene; Keith, meanwhile, was practically bubbly. 'Being a Stoic is really a very uncomfortable position to be in!', he declared merrily. 'People throughout history have made this big mistake about happiness, and here we are, the Stoics, standing out on the fringe – beyond the fringe, really! – and shouting from over the horizon: "You've got it all wrong! You've got it all wrong!"'

Keith traced his beginnings as a Stoic to a bizarre incident that had happened to him at around the age of twenty, while he was walking through a wooded park not far from his home outside London. He described it as a shift in perspective – the kind of jolting insight that often gets described as a 'spiritual experience'. 'It was quite a short thing,' he recalled. 'Just a minute or two. But suddenly, for that minute or two, I was . . . ' He paused, hunting for the right words. 'I was *directly aware of how everything was connected together in space and time*,' he said at last. 'It was like travelling out into space, perceiving the universe as a whole, and seeing everything connected together in exactly the way it was meant to be. As something finished and complete.'

I took a sip of Diet Coke, and waited.

'It was like an Airfix model,' he said, with an exasperated shake of the head, which I took to mean that it hadn't really been like an Airfix model at all. 'I had the sense that it was all done *on purpose*, by some kind of agency. Not a God outside the universe, pulling the strings, you understand. But as if *the whole thing itself* were God.' He paused again. 'You know, the funny thing is, it didn't really strike me as particularly significant at the time.' Having briefly entered a mystic realm of cosmic consciousness, the twenty-year-old Seddon forgot about it, went home, and got on with his degree.

But after a while, the memory of those two minutes began to gnaw at him. He read the *Tao Te Ching*, looking for clues in Taoism. He explored Buddhism. But ultimately it was Stoicism that spoke to him. 'It just seemed so much more solid and down-to-earth,' he said. 'I thought: "There's nothing here that I can argue with!"' His vision in the park, it turned out, mirrored the Stoics' own idiosyncratic form of religious belief. They too held that the universe was God – that there was a grand plan, and that everything was happening for a reason. The Stoic goal of acting according to reason meant acting in accordance with this universal plan. 'Constantly regard the universe as one living being, having one substance and one soul,' says Marcus Aurelius. 'Whatever happens at all, happens as it should.' To modern secularist minds, this is certainly the part of Stoicism that is hardest to swallow. Calling the universe 'God' might be just about acceptable; that's arguably only a matter of language. But to suggest that it's all heading somewhere, in accordance with a plan, is far more problematic. Indeed, Keith explained with a sigh, he was always having to quell fractious arguments between atheist Stoics and theist Stoics on the International Stoic Forum – though as a good Stoic, naturally he didn't let it upset him all that much.

You don't necessarily need to accept the Stoic notion of a 'grand plan', however, in order to embrace its flip side, which is much more important to Stoicism in everyday life: that whether or not there is some agency bigger than ourselves, controlling the way things unfold, each one of us clearly has very little *individual* control over the universe. Keith and Jocelyn had learned this the hard way. They would have preferred to live without Jocelyn's arthritis, without Keith's constant fatigue, and with more money. But without their ever requesting it, circumstances had taught them Stoicism's central insight about control, and about the wisdom of understanding the limits of your own.

As Seneca frequently observes, we habitually act as if our control over the world were much greater than it really is. Even such personal matters as our health, our finances, and our reputations are ultimately beyond our control; we can try to influence them, of course, but frequently things won't go our way. And the behaviour of other people is even further beyond our control. For most conventional notions of happiness – which consist in making things the way you want them to be – this poses a big problem. In better times, it's easy to forget how little we control: we can usually manage to convince ourselves that we attained the promotion at work, or the new relationship, or the Nobel Prize, thanks solely to our own brilliance and effort. But unhappy times bring home the truth of the matter. Jobs are lost; plans go wrong; people die. If your strategy for happiness depends on bending circumstances to your will, this is terrible news: the best you can do is to pray that not all that much will go wrong and try to distract yourself when it does. For the Stoics, however, tranquility entails confronting the reality of your limited control. 'Never have I trusted Fortune,' writes Seneca, 'even when she seemed to be at peace. All her generous bounties – money, office, influence – I deposited where she could ask for them back without disturbing me.' Those things lie beyond the individual's control; if you invest your happiness in them, you're setting yourself up for a rude shock. The only things we can truly control, the Stoics argue, are our *judgments* – what we believe – about our circumstances. But this isn't bad news. From the Stoic perspective, as we've already seen, our judgments are what cause our distress – and so they're all that we need to be able to control in order to substitute serenity for suffering.

'Suppose somebody insults you – insults you *really* obnoxiously,' Keith said, leaning forward in his armchair as he warmed to his theme. 'The Stoic, if he's a good enough Stoic, isn't going to get annoyed or angry or upset or disconcerted, because he'll see that, ultimately, nothing bad has happened. To get annoyed, he would first have to have judged that the other person had harmed him. The trouble is that you're conditioned into making that kind of judgment all your life.'

This is a relatively small example: it's easy enough to see that a verbal insult need entail no personal harm. It would be vastly harder to make the same argument about, say, the death of a friend. This is why the notion of a 'grand plan' is ultimately so crucial to a thoroughgoing embrace of Stoicism: it's only by seeing death as part of such a plan that one could one ever hope to feel serene about it. 'Do not despise death, but be well content with it, since this too is one of those things which nature wills,' says Marcus. But this is a tall order. The best that Stoicism could do for an atheist, in this situation, would probably be to help her see that she retained *some* control over her judgments. She might be able to remind herself that it was possible to choose to be seriously but reasonably upset, instead of spiralling into utter despair.

Yet this hardly invalidates the usefulness of a Stoic approach when it comes to more minor, everyday forms of distress, which is where Seddon advised his correspondence-course students to begin. Try thinking Stoically, he told them, for the duration of a single trip to the supermarket. Is something out of stock? Are the queues too long? The Stoic isn't necessarily obliged to tolerate the situation; he might decide to switch to another store instead. But to become upset would be, in Stoic terms, an error of judgment. You cannot control the situation, so reacting with fury against that reality is irrational. Your irritation, moreover, is almost certainly out of all proportion to the actual harm – if any – that has been done to you by the inconvenience; there are no grounds for taking it personally. Maybe it's an opportunity to engage in the 'premeditation of evils': what's the absolute worst that could happen as a result of this? Almost always, asking this question will reveal your judgments about the situation to have been exaggerated, and cutting them down to size will vastly increase your chances of replacing distress or annoyance with calm.

It is essential to grasp a distinction here between acceptance and resignation: using your powers of reason to stop being disturbed by a situation doesn't mean you shouldn't try to change it. To take one very obvious example, a Stoic who finds herself in an abusive relationship would not be expected to put up with it, and would almost certainly be best advised to take action to leave it. Her Stoicism would oblige her only to confront the truth of her situation – to see it for what it was – and then to take whatever actions were within her power, instead of railing against her circumstances as if they ought not exist. 'The cucumber is bitter? Put it down,' Marcus advises. 'There are brambles in the path? Step to one side. That is enough, without also asking: "How did these things come into the world at all?"'

Or take somebody who had been wrongly convicted and imprisoned, said Keith. 'Now, that person, as a Stoic, is going to say that having been unjustly imprisoned, in one sense, *doesn't actually matter*. What matters is how I engage with the situation. Now that I'm here, rather than anywhere else, here in this time and this place – what can I do? Maybe I need to read up on the law and appeal my case and fight for my freedom. That's certainly not resignation. But, rationally, I'm accepting the reality of the situation. And then I don't need to feel distressed by a judgment that it ought not to be happening. Because it *is* happening.' For Keith and Jocelyn, this struck close to home. 'Without Stoicism,' he said quietly, gesturing at his wife and himself, 'I really don't see how we'd have been able to keep going through this.'

Later, as I headed back out into the Watford dusk, I had the sense of having absorbed some of Keith's rigorously rational tranquility, as if by osmosis. Back in London, buying food to make dinner for the friends with whom I was staying, I did indeed find myself at the wrong end of a long supermarket queue, attended by one overworked member of staff and a row of malfunctioning self-service machines. I felt a flash of irritation, before I managed to call the Stoics to mind. The situation was what it was. I could leave if I chose to. And the worst-case scenario here – a few minutes' delay before my friends and I could eat – was so trifling as to be laughable. My irrational judgments were the problem, not the supermarket queue. I felt disproportionately pleased with myself for recognising this. True, in the long history of Stoicism, it was a pretty minor triumph. It didn't really compare, for example, to staying tranquil while being forced to commit suicide by bleeding oneself to death, like Seneca. Still, I told myself – Stoically – you had to start somewhere.

For the Stoics, then, our judgments about the world are all that we can control, but also all that we need to control in order to be happy; tranquility results from replacing our irrational judgments with rational ones. And dwelling on the worst-case scenario, the 'premeditation of evils', is often the best way to achieve this – even to the point, Seneca suggests, of deliberately experiencing those 'evils', so as to grasp that they might not be as bad as you'd irrationally feared.

It was this last technique that was to prove especially inspiring, centuries later, to a maverick psychotherapist named Albert Ellis, who did more than anyone else to restore Stoicism to the forefront of modern psychology. In 2006, in the final months of Ellis's life, I went to visit him, in a cramped top-floor apartment above the establishment that he had named – with characteristic disregard for modesty – the Albert Ellis Institute, in uptown Manhattan. He was ninety-three and did not get out of bed for the interview; to accommodate his severe deafness, he wore a chunky pair of headphones, and demanded that I speak into a microphone. 'As the Buddha said two and a half thousand years ago,' he said, soon after we'd started talking, and jabbing a finger in my direction, 'we're all out of our fucking minds! That's just the way we are.' To be honest, I would have felt short-changed if he hadn't used such language early in our conversation, such was his notoriety for swearing. But I knew he had more going for him than entertainment value. A couple of decades previously, America's psychologists had voted him the second most influential psychotherapist of the twentieth century, behind the founder of humanistic psychology, Carl Rogers, but – amazingly – ahead of Sigmund Freud. This was especially generous of them in view of Ellis's opinion of much of the world of conventional psychology, which was that it was 'horseshit'.

In the 1950s, when Ellis first began to promote his Stoic-flavoured view of psychology, it was deeply controversial, at odds both with self-help's focus on positive thinking and with the Freudianism that dominated the profession. On several occasions, at psychology conferences, he'd been jeered. But now, with more than fifty books to his name – one typical bestseller was entitled *How to Stubbornly Refuse to Make Yourself Miserable About Anything, Yes, Anything!* – he exuded the satisfaction of intellectual victory.

A few days before, I had witnessed Ellis deliver one of his famous 'Friday night workshops', in which he hauled volunteers on stage in order to berate them, for their own benefit, in front of an audience of trainee therapists and interested members of the public. The first participant I watched had been beset by anxiety: she couldn't decide whether to give up her job and move across the country to join her long-term boyfriend. She wanted to marry him, and she didn't much like her job, but what if he wasn't the one for her? 'So maybe he turns out to be a jerk, and you get divorced!' Ellis shouted – because he was deaf, but also, I suspected, because he enjoyed shouting. 'That would be highly disagreeable! You might feel sad! But it doesn't have to be *awful*. It doesn't have to be *completely terrible*.'

This distinction – between outcomes that are completely terrible, versus those that are merely bad – might sound glib, or like a trivial quibble over vocabulary. To understand why it is neither, and why it goes to the heart of Ellis's outlook on the virtues of negative thinking, it is necessary to return to his youth, in Pittsburgh, in the first decades of the twentieth century. From an early age, thinking like a Stoic proved an urgent personal necessity for Ellis. His mother, as he remembered her, was self-absorbed and melodramatic; his father, a travelling salesman, was rarely around. At the age of five, Ellis developed severe kidney problems, condemning him to long stays in hospital throughout his childhood, during which his parents almost never visited. Alone with his thoughts, he drifted into philosophical speculations on the nature of existence and eventually read Seneca's *Letters from a Stoic*. The Stoics' focus on the importance of one's judgments about one's circumstances struck a chord; his unhappy existence, he came to see, might prove a surprisingly useful crucible in which to develop Stoic wisdom. And so, by 1932, when he was a gangly eighteen-year-old with a crippling fear of speaking to women, he knew enough philosophy and psychology to try addressing his shyness problem by means of a practical Stoic experiment. One day that summer – the summer that Amelia Earhart flew the Atlantic and that Walt Disney released the first Technicolor cartoon movie – Ellis arrived at the Bronx Botanical Garden, near his home in New York City, to put his plan into practice.

Every day for a month, Ellis had decided, he would follow an unbreakable rule. He would take up a position on a park bench, and, if a woman sat down near him, he would attempt to strike up an innocuous conversation. That was all. He ended up sharing benches, and attempting conversation, with a hundred and thirty women. 'Whereupon thirty got up and walked away,' he recalled, years later. 'But that left me with a sample of a hundred, which was good enough for research purposes. I spoke to the whole hundred – for the first time in my life.' Only in one case did the conversation progress far enough for Ellis and his benchmate to make a plan to meet again – 'and she didn't show up'. To an uninformed observer, the experiment might have looked like an utter failure. But Ellis would probably have rejected any such verdict as 'horseshit'; for him, it had been a triumphant success.

What Ellis had grasped about his unstated beliefs concerning conversation with women – an insight he would later extend to the beliefs that lie behind all instances of worry or anxiety – is that they were absolutist. To put it another way, it wasn't just that he *wanted* to be less shy, and that he *wanted* to be able to talk to women. Rather, he had been operating under the absolutist conviction that he *needed* their approval. Later, he would coin a name for this habit of mind: 'musturbation'. We elevate those things we want, those things we would prefer to have, into things we believe we *must* have; we feel we *must* perform well in certain circumstances or that other people *must* treat us well. Because we think these things must occur, it follows that it would be an absolute catastrophe if they did not. No wonder we get so anxious: we've decided that if we failed to meet our goal it wouldn't merely be bad, but completely bad – absolutely terrible.

Ellis's encounters in the Bronx Botanical Garden had shown him that the worst-case scenario – rejection – was far from the absolute disaster he had been fearing. 'Nobody took out a stiletto and cut my balls off,' he remembered. 'Nobody vomited and ran away. Nobody called the cops.' It was actually a good thing, Stoically speaking, that none of his conversations had ended in thrilling dates; if he had achieved such a spectacular result, it might subtly have reinforced his irrational beliefs about the awfulness of *not* achieving them. This 'shame-attacking exercise', as he later came to refer to these kinds of undertakings, was the 'premeditation of evils' rendered real and immediate. The worst thing about any event, Ellis liked to say, 'is usually your exaggerated belief in its horror'. The way to defuse that belief was to confront the reality – and in reality, getting rejected by women turned out to be merely undesirable, not horrifying or terrible. Later, as a working psychotherapist, Ellis devised other shame-attacking exercises; in one, he sent his clients onto the streets of Manhattan with instructions to approach strangers and to say to them: 'Excuse me, I just got out of the lunatic asylum – can you tell me what year it is?' It showed the clients that being thought of as crazy wouldn't kill them. In another, he instructed people to take rides on the New York City subway, calling out loud the names of the stations. When he told me about this, I replied that I thought I'd find such an exercise paralysingly embarrassing. Ellis said that was exactly why I should try it.

Explaining the difference between a *terrible* outcome and a merely *undesirable* one became a governing mission of Ellis's career. He went so far as to insist that nothing at all could ever be absolutely terrible – 'because', he wrote, 'when you insist that an undesirable event is awful or terrible, you are implying, if you're honest with yourself, that it is as bad as it could be.' Yet nothing could be 100 per cent bad, he argued, because it could always conceivably be worse. Even if one were murdered, 'that is very bad, but not one hundred per cent bad,' because several of your loved ones could meet the same fate, 'and that would be worse. If you are tortured to death slowly, you could always be tortured to death slower.' He did grudgingly concede that there was one event that might legitimately be viewed as 100 per cent bad: the complete destruction of absolutely everything on the planet. But that, he pointed out, 'hardly seems likely in the near future'.

This might seem like a bizarrely cold-hearted attitude to take towards such things as torture or murder; it seems tasteless to try to construct elaborate hypothetical scenarios merely to find something that could be worse than them. But it is precisely in the context of such extremely undesirable scenarios, Ellis insisted, that the strategy of focusing on the worst-case scenario – and distinguishing between *very bad* and *completely terrible* events – really comes into its own. It turns infinite fears into finite ones. One of his clients, he recalled, found herself unable to pursue a romantic life because of an extreme fear that she might contract AIDS from kissing, or even from shaking hands. If a friend suffered from such an anxiety, your first response might be reassurance: pointing out, in other words, how extremely unlikely it was that this scenario would ever occur. That was Ellis's first response, too. But, as we've seen, reassurance carries a sting: reassuring the woman that her fears were unlikely to come true did nothing to dislodge her belief that it would be unimaginably bad if they did. And so Ellis switched to negative visualisation instead. Suppose you did get AIDS, he said. That would be pretty bad. But absolutely horrific, or 100 per cent terrible? Obviously not: one could imagine worse scenarios. One always can. And one could imagine still finding sources of happiness in life, despite having contracted AIDS. The distinction between judging something to be 'very bad' and judging it to be 'absolutely horrific' makes all the difference in the world. It is only to the absolutely horrific that we respond with blind terror; all other fears are finite, and thus susceptible to being coped with. Grasping this at last, Ellis's client was able to stop fearing an inconceivably terrible calamity, and instead begin taking normal precautions to avoid a highly undesirable, though also highly unlikely, worst-case scenario. Moreover, she had internalised the

Stoic understanding that it was not within her control to eliminate all possibility of the fate that she feared. 'If you accept that the universe is uncontrollable,' Ellis told me, 'you're going to be a lot less anxious.'

Such Stoic insights served Ellis especially well in the months after I met him. His final days were afflicted not only by intestinal problems and pneumonia, but by a dispute with the other directors of the Institute. They fired him from the board, cancelled his Friday night workshops, and stopped paying for his accommodation, forcing him to move out. He sued, a judge ruled in his favour, and by the time of his death he was back in his apartment. True to his principles, he insisted that the contretemps had never made him upset. It was all highly undesirable, of course, but not horrific, and there was no point insisting that the entire universe fall in line with his wishes. The other members of the board, he told one reporter, were 'fucked-up, fallible human beings – just like everyone else'.

'Chancery Lane.'

I speak the words out loud, but in such a nervous croak that I'm not sure anybody hears them. Glancing up and down the carriage, I can't see any evidence of anyone having noticed. Then the middle-aged man sitting opposite me glances up from his newspaper, with an expression I can only describe as one of mild interest. I meet his eye for a moment, then look away. Nothing else happens. The train stops. Some people get off. Suddenly, it occurs to me that I have subconsciously been expecting something calamitous to happen – an explosion of ridicule, at least. Now that it hasn't, I feel disoriented.

As we approach Holborn, I say 'Holborn' – louder this time,

and less tremulously. The same man looks up. A baby two seats away stares at me, open-mouthed, but would probably have done so anyway.

It is at Tottenham Court Road that I cross some kind of psychic boundary. The adrenaline subsides, the panic dissipates, and I find myself confronting the very truth that Albert Ellis's Stoical shame-attacking experiment had been designed to beat into my brain: that none of this is anywhere near as bad as I'd been anticipating. I have been left with no option but to see that my fear of embarrassment was based on profoundly irrational ideas about how terrible it would be if people thought badly of me. The truth is that they aren't being outwardly mocking or hostile at all – mainly, no doubt, because they're much too busy thinking about themselves. At Tottenham Court Road, a few more people look my way when I speak. But I don't care anymore. I feel invincible.

Three stations further on, at Marble Arch, I get up and leave the train, beaming to myself, suffused with Stoic serenity. Nobody in the carriage seems particularly interested in that, either.

3

The Storm Before the Calm

A Buddhist Guide to Not Thinking Positively

You want it to be one way. But it's the other way.
                              – Marlo Stanfield in *The Wire*

IN THE EARLY 1960S, Robert Aitken, an American Zen Buddhist living in Hawaii, began to notice something inexplicable and alarming. Aitken was one of the pioneers in bringing Buddhism to the spiritually hungry West, and at their home in Honolulu, he and his wife Anne had opened a *zendo*, or meditation centre, catering mainly to the island's growing population of hippies. But something about a number of the new meditation students didn't seem right. They would arrive and sit down on their cushions at the appointed time, where they would remain still as stones, apparently meditating; but then, when the bell rang to signal the end of a meditation period, they would rise to their feet – and immediately collapse onto the ground. It took Aitken several weeks of tactful enquiries to establish what was going on. Word had got around, among the hippies of Honolulu, that attempting Zen meditation while under the influence of LSD was the ultimate trip, an express train to mind-blowing ecstasy.

As the craze for Buddhist meditation spread further through America and Europe, the notion that it was a shortcut to ecstasy proved a popular one. Back in the 1950s, that had certainly been what had appealed to Jack Kerouac, who embraced it with an enthusiasm he otherwise reserved for whisky and magic mushrooms. Blood circulation problems meant that it caused him agony to sit cross-legged for more than a few minutes at a time, but he battled on anyway, determined to penetrate new realms of bliss. Sometimes, it even seemed to work. 'Fall, hands a-clasped, into instantaneous ecstasy like a shot of heroin or morphine,' he wrote to his friend Allen Ginsberg, describing his early efforts. 'The glands inside my brain discharging the good glad fluid (Holy Fluid) . . . healing all my sickness . . . erasing all . . . ' More often, though, his knees simply hurt too much, and after a short time he would be forced, as one Kerouac biographer notes, 'to scramble to his feet and rub his legs to restore circulation'.

These days, the more prevalent stereotype about meditation is that it is a path not to ecstasy but to trance-like calm. It sometimes seems impossible to open a magazine, or a newspaper features section, without being preached to about the relaxation-inducing benefits of mindfulness meditation. The stock photograph most commonly used to illustrate such articles is of a woman in a leotard, on a beach; her legs are crossed and her eyes closed, and an insipid smile is playing on her lips. (If the topic of the article is 'using meditation in everyday life', it's sometimes a man or woman in a business suit, instead – same cross-legged posture, same smile.) The Australian meditation teacher Paul Wilson, the bestselling self-styled 'guru of calm', has done much to reinforce this stereotype: his books on meditation include *The Calm Technique, Instant Calm, The Little Book of Calm, The Big*

Book of Calm, Calm at Work, Calm Mother, Calm Child, The Complete Book of Calm and *Calm for Life.*

The idea of meditation as a path to calmness is somewhat more realistic, since calmness – unlike unbroken ecstasy – can indeed be one of its side effects. Yet all these associations have contributed to a modern image of meditation as a sophisticated form of positive thinking, which is almost the opposite of the truth. In fact, meditation has little to do with achieving any specific desired state of mind, no matter whether blissful or calm. At Buddhism's core, instead, is an often misunderstood notion that is starkly opposed to most contemporary assumptions about how to be happy, and that places it squarely on the 'negative path' to happiness: non-attachment.

At the root of all suffering, says the second of the four 'noble truths' that define Buddhism, is attachment. The fact that we desire some things, and dislike or hate others, is what motivates virtually every human activity. Rather than merely enjoying pleasurable things during the moments in which they occur, and experiencing the unpleasantness of painful things, we develop the habits of clinging and aversion: we grasp at what we like, trying to hold on to it forever, and push away what we don't like, trying to avoid it at all costs. Both constitute attachment. Pain is inevitable, from this perspective, but *suffering* is an optional extra, resulting from our attachments, which represent our attempt to try to deny the unavoidable truth that everything is impermanent. Develop a strong attachment to your good looks – as opposed to merely enjoying them while they last – and you will suffer when they fade, as they inevitably will; develop a strong attachment to your luxurious lifestyle, and your life may become an unhappy, fearful struggle to keep things that way. Attach too strongly to life, and death will seem all the more frightening. (The parallels here with

Stoicism, and with Albert Ellis's distinction between what we prefer and what we feel we must have, aren't coincidental; the traditions overlap in countless ways.) Non-attachment need not mean withdrawing from life, or suppressing natural impulses, or engaging in punishing self-denial. It simply means approaching the whole of life – inner thoughts and emotions, outer events and circumstances – without clinging or aversion. To live non-attachedly is to feel impulses, think thoughts, and experience life without becoming hooked by mental narratives about how things 'should' be, or should never be, or should remain forever. The perfectly non-attached Buddhist would be simply, calmly present, and non-judgmentally aware.

Which, let's be frank, isn't going to happen for most of us any time soon. The idea of living without wanting things to be one way rather than another way strikes most people as a strange sort of goal. How could you not be attached to having good friends, to enjoying fulfilling relationships, or to doing well for yourself materially? And how could you be happy if you weren't thus attached? Meditation might indeed be the path to non-attachment, as the Buddhists claim – but it is by no means clear, to anyone accustomed to the standard approaches to happiness, why that's a destination that one might ever wish to reach.

What first led me to question this commonsense position was the title of a slim book by another American Zen Buddhist and trained psychiatrist. It was called *Ending the Pursuit of Happiness*, and its author, a man named Barry Magid, argued that the idea of using meditation to make your life 'better' or 'happier', in any conventional sense, was a misunderstanding. The point, instead, was to learn how to stop trying to fix things, to stop being so preoccupied with trying to control one's experience of the world, to *give up* trying to replace unpleasant thoughts and emotions with more pleasant ones, and to see that, through dropping the 'pursuit of happiness', a more profound peace might result. Or, rather, that wasn't the 'point', exactly, because Magid objected to the notion that meditation had a point. If it did, he seemed to imply, that would make it just another happiness technique, a way of satisfying our desire to cling to certain states and eliminate others. This was all deeply confusing. What would be the point, I wondered, of doing something pointless? Why would anyone try to end the pursuit of happiness, if not to become happy – in which case, wouldn't they still be pursuing happiness, only by more cunning means?

Barry Magid practised psychiatry in a large, sparsely furnished room on the ground floor of an apartment block near Central Park, on the Upper West Side of Manhattan. It was unlit save for a desk lamp, and its two leather chairs were placed unusually far from each other, against opposite walls, so that Magid's head seemed to loom out at me from the dark. He was a tall, owlish man in his early sixties, with wire-rimmed glasses, and when I asked him a rambling question about Buddhism and non-attachment, he looked at me with mild amusement. Then he started talking about something else entirely.

What I really needed to understand, he told me, was the myth of Oedipus. In Magid's view, the famous tale of the ancient Greek king – who kills his father and marries his mother, bringing disaster to his family and his city, and prompting him to gouge out his eyes – was the perfect metaphor for what was wrong with pursuing happiness. This had little to do with the 'Oedipus complex', Freud's theory about boys secretly wanting to have sex with their mothers. The real message of the myth, Magid explained, was that struggling to escape your demons was what gave them their power. It was the 'backwards law' in mythological form: clinging to a particular version of a happy life, while fighting to eliminate all possibility of an unhappy one, was the cause of the problem, not its solution.

You may be familiar with the story. When Oedipus is born to the King and Queen of Thebes, his horrible fate – that he will kill one parent and marry the other – has already been foretold by an oracle. His mother and father, desperate to ensure that this never comes to pass, persuade a local shepherd to take the newborn, with instructions to abandon him to the elements. But the shepherd can't bring himself to let Oedipus die; the child lives, and subsequently becomes the adoptive son of the King and Queen of Corinth. But when Oedipus confronts them, some time later, with the rumour that he is adopted, they deny it – so when he hears about the oracle's terrible prophecy, he assumes that they are the parents to whom it refers. Resolving to escape the curse by putting as much distance as possible between himself and the couple he takes to be his parents, Oedipus travels far away. Unfortunately, the faraway place at which he arrives is Thebes. Thereafter, fate drags him to his inevitable end: first, he becomes involved in an unlikely dispute over a chariot, and kills its occupant, who turns out to have been his father. Then he falls in love with his mother.

One obvious reading of this myth is that you can never escape your fate, no matter how hard you try. But Magid preferred another. 'The quintessential point,' he told me, 'is that if you flee it, it'll come back to bite you. The very thing from which you're in flight – well, it's the fleeing that brings on the problem. For Freud, our whole psychology is organised around this avoidance. The unconscious is the repository of everything that we're avoiding.'

The founding myth of Buddhism is practically a mirror-image of all this. The Buddha becomes psychologically free – enlightened

– by confronting negativity, suffering and impermanence, rather than struggling to avoid them. According to legend, the historical Buddha was born Siddharta Gautama, the son of a king, in a palace in the foothills of the Himalayas. As was the case with Oedipus, his destiny had been foretold: it was prophesied that he would become either a powerful king or a holy man. In common with parents throughout history, Siddharta's preferred the job description that came with good pay and security, and so they dedicated themselves to making sure their son would grow to love privilege. They made his life a luxurious prison, pampering him with fine foods and armies of servants; he even managed to marry and have a son without once leaving his bubble of entitlement. It was only at the age of twenty-nine that he managed to venture outside the compound. There, he saw what have become enshrined in Buddhist lore as the 'Four Sights': an old man, a sick man, a corpse, and a wandering ascetic monk. The first three symbolised the inevitability of impermanence, and the three fates awaiting us all. Siddharta was shocked into abandoning his comfortable life, and his family, to become an itinerant monk. It was in India, some years later, that he is supposed to have achieved enlightenment after spending the night sitting beneath a fig tree, thereby becoming the Buddha, 'the one who woke up'. But it was those initial sights, according to the myth, that first awoke his understanding of impermanence. Buddhism's path to serenity began with a confrontation with the negative.

From Barry Magid's Buddhist–Freudian point of view, then, most people who thought they were 'seeking happiness' were really running away from things of which they were barely aware. Meditation, the way he described it, was a way to stop running. You sat still, and watched your thoughts and emotions and desires and aversions come and go, and you resisted the urge to try to flee from them, to fix them, or to cling to them. You practised non-attachment, in other words. Whatever came up, negative or positive, you stayed present and observed it. It wasn't about escaping into ecstasy – or even into calmness, as the word is normally understood; and it certainly wasn't about positive thinking. It was about the significantly greater challenge of declining to do any of that.

It was shortly after meeting Magid that I took the rash decision to spend almost a week with forty strangers, meditating for about nine hours a day, in the middle of a forest, in the depths of winter, many miles from the nearest town, in almost unbroken silence.

Which proved interesting.

'The basic meditation instruction is really incredibly simple,' said Howard, one of the two teachers charged with running the retreat at the Insight Meditation Society, a converted turn-of-the-century mansion in the remote pine forests of central Massachusetts. It was early evening, and all forty of us were seated on cushions filled with buckwheat hulls in the building's austere main hall, listening to a man with a voice so calming it was impossible to imagine an instruction he might give that you wouldn't be lulled into following. 'Sit comfortably, gently close your eyes, and notice the breath as it flows in and out. You can focus on this sensation at the nostrils, or at the abdomen. Just follow one breath in, and one breath out. And then do it again.' There were nervous chuckles; surely it wasn't going to be that simple, or that boring? 'Other things will come up,' Howard continued. 'Physical sensations, feelings and thoughts will carry us away into distraction. In meditation, when we notice that happening, we don't judge. We just return to the breath.' It really was that simple, apparently. What he failed to point out – though we were to discover it soon enough – was that 'simple' didn't mean 'easy'.

I had arrived at the Insight Meditation Society earlier that afternoon, sharing a taxi from the nearest major railway station, about twenty-five miles away, with an Israeli student I'll call Adina. As we bounced along uneven backwoods roads, she explained that she was attending the retreat because she felt lost. 'It's like I have no roots anywhere . . . nothing to hold on to, no structure in my life,' she said. I couldn't help wincing inwardly at her candour: we'd only just met, and as far as I was concerned this was over-sharing. But what she said next made sense. She was hoping that meditation might be a way not to stop feeling lost, but to come to see the lostness differently – to embrace it, even. The American Buddhist nun Pema Chödrön calls this 'relaxing into the ground-lessness of our situation', and it harmonises well with the idea of non-attachment. Chödrön suggests that 'groundlessness' is actually everyone's situation, all the time, whether they like it or not. It's just that most of us can't relax in the presence of that truth; instead, we frantically scramble to deny it.

Our taxi driver seemed lost in a more literal sense, plunging down rutted tracks through the forest, then reversing back up them again, cursing his satellite navigation system. The meditation centre proved seriously hard to find, which wasn't surprising; isolation was the point. When we finally arrived, I was shown to my room – a narrow, monkish cell, looking out over miles of uninterrupted forest. It contained a single bed, a sink, a small wardrobe, a shelf, and nothing else. I stowed my suitcase under my bed and hurried to the main hall, where a staff member outlined the week's ground rules. We would be expected to spend one hour a day helping to clean the building, or prepare food, or do the dishes, she explained. In a few moments' time, she would

ring the small brass gong on the building's central staircase, and
we would be expected to fall silent – with only a handful of
exceptions, including emergencies and question-and-answer
sessions with the teachers – for the rest of the retreat. Since we
wouldn't be speaking, she added, it would be best if we kept our
eyes downcast, too, so as to avoid the temptation to spend the
week communicating via smiling, scowling, and winking. There
would be no alcohol, no sex, no use of telephones or the internet,
no listening to music, and also no reading or writing – since these,
she said, could rupture one's interior quiet as surely as audible
conversation. Then again, as the daily schedule we found pinned
to the noticeboard made clear, there would be no time for any
of that, anyway:

5.30 a.m. – *Waking bell*

6.00 a.m. – *Sitting meditation*

6.30 a.m. – *Breakfast*

7.15 a.m. – *Work period (kitchen cleaning, food preparation, etc.)*

8.15 a.m. – *Sitting meditation*

9.15 a.m. – *Walking meditation*

10.00 a.m. – *Sitting meditation*

10.45 a.m. – *Walking meditation*

11.30 a.m. – *Sitting meditation*

12.00 noon – *Lunch, followed by rest*

1.45 p.m. – *Walking meditation*

2.15 p.m. – *Sitting meditation*

3.00 p.m. – *Walking meditation*

3.45 p.m. – *Sitting meditation*

4.30 p.m. – *Walking meditation*

5.00 p.m. – *Light meal*

6.15 p.m. – *Sitting meditation*

7.00 p.m. – Walking meditation
7.30 p.m. – Dharma talk
8.30 p.m. – Walking meditation
9.00 p.m. – Sitting meditation
9.30 p.m. – Sleep or further meditation

'Well, that'll be the structure you were looking for,' I said to Adina, who was standing nearby. The moment I'd said this, it struck me as an annoying, smart-aleck kind of remark. What made it worse, somehow, was that it was the last thing I said. A few seconds later, we heard the deep ring of the gong, and silence descended.

It didn't take very long on the meditation cushion, however, to discover that outer silence did not automatically confer inner silence. For the first several hours after receiving the basic instructions – the rest of the first evening, and most of the following morning – my mind was occupied almost exclusively by song lyrics, looping loudly on repeat. Inexplicably, and appallingly, they were mostly the lyrics to the 1997 song 'Barbie Girl', by the Danish-Norwegian kitsch-pop group Aqua, a track I had always despised. The music was interrupted only by occasional anxious thoughts about how I was going to make it through the week, plus stray entries from my to-do list that I'd forgotten to deal with prior to my departure.

In my defence, this – the mental chatter in general, not 'Barbie Girl' – is almost everybody's first experience of silent meditation. When you eliminate the distractions of external noise, and turn your attention inwards, what strikes you first is this: it's almost constantly noisy in there. It's not that the inner chatter is somehow generated by the attempt to meditate. It's simply that outer noise, the rest of the time, drowns out the inner noise; in the silence of the forest and the meditation hall, it all became suddenly audible. 'One realises', as the spiritual teacher Jiddu Krishnamurti once put it, 'that one's brain is constantly chattering, constantly planning, designing: what it will do, what it has done, the past impinging itself on the present. It is everlasting chattering, chattering, chattering.'

An understandable response to such chatter, when you're attempting to meditate, is to try to quieten it – to dampen it down, or perhaps even to try to stop thinking altogether. But one central principle of *vipassana* meditation, the variety taught at the Insight Meditation Society, is the opposite: to let the clamour be. As the Buddhist teacher Steve Hagen says in his pithy guidebook *Meditation: Now or Never*, 'we do not try to forcefully detach ourselves from the feelings, thoughts and expectations that arise in our mind. We don't try to force anything into or out of the mind. Rather, we let things rise and fall, come and go, and simply be . . . there will be times in meditation when we're relaxed, and times when our minds are agitated. We do not seek to attain a relaxed state, or to drive out our agitated and distracted mind. That is just more agitation.' This is the first big step towards nonattachment: learning to view passing thoughts and feelings as if one were a spectator, not a participant. Consider it too closely, and this idea becomes dizzying, given that watching your own thought processes is itself a thought process; it can be easy to feel caught in some kind of infinite loop.

Fortunately, it isn't necessary to resolve this conundrum in order to practise meditation. The technique, as Howard had explained, is simply to return – every time you realise you've been carried away by a narrative or by an emotion – to the breath. The following evening, during the teachers' daily talk, he quoted the Catholic mystic St Francis de Sales, a practitioner of Christian meditation: 'Bring yourself back to the point quite gently. And even if you do nothing during the whole of your hour but bring your heart back a thousand times, though it went away every time you brought it back, your hour would be very well employed.' There is more to non-attachment than this – and much more, it's worth emphasising, to Buddhism than non-attachment. But it is where it all begins.

It becomes easier to make sense of this when you realise that Buddhism, though we think of it today as a religion, was originally just as much an approach to the study of psychology. The central Buddhist psychological text, the *Abhidhamma*, is a ferociously complex tome of lists and sub-clauses and technical argument. But one of its more straightforward insights is the notion that the mind can be viewed, in many respects, as one of the senses – like seeing, hearing, smell, touch, and taste. Just as we receive smells through the 'sense-door' of the nose, and tastes through the sense-door of the tongue, it's possible to see the mind as a kind of sense-door, too, or as a screen on which thoughts are projected, like images in a cinema. This isn't how we usually think about thinking. Sounds and smells and tastes, after all, are just sounds and smells and tastes, but thoughts, we tend to assume, are something much more important. Because they come from within us, they feel more essential, and expressive of our deepest selves. But is that true, really? When you start meditating, it soon becomes apparent that thoughts – and emotions – bubble up in much the same uncontrollable, unbidden fashion in which noises reach the ears, smells reach the nose, and so on. I could no more choose for thoughts not to occur than I could choose not to feel chilly when I was woken by the ringing of the morning bell at five-thirty each day – or, for that matter, than I could choose not to hear the bell.

Seeing thoughts as similar to the other five senses makes

non-attachment seem much more approachable as a goal. In the analogy most commonly used by contemporary Buddhists, mental activity begins to seem more like weather – like clouds and sunny spells, rainstorms and blizzards, arising and passing away. The mind, in this analogy, is the sky, and the sky doesn't cling to specific weather conditions, nor try to get rid of the 'bad' ones. The sky just is. In this the Buddhists go further than the Stoics, who can sometimes seem rather attached to certain mind-states, especially that of tranquility. The perfect Stoic adapts his or her thinking so as to remain undisturbed by undesirable circum- stances; the perfect Buddhist sees thinking itself as just another set of circumstances, to be non-judgmentally observed.

Even more challenging than practising non-attachment to passing thoughts and feelings is practising it in the presence of physical pain; to be non-judgmental about being in agony seems preposterous. But it is here that some of the most powerful scientific evidence for cultivating non-attachment has been accumulating in recent years. Some Buddhists, such as Barry Magid, might object to the implication that the benefits of meditation need to be scientifically 'proven'. But the science is intriguing nonetheless – especially in the case of a series of experiments conducted in 2009, at the University of North Carolina, by a young psychologist named Fadel Zeidan.

Zeidan wanted to test the effects of meditation on people's ability to endure physical pain, and so, with refreshing straight- forwardness, he decided to hurt them. His research employed mild electric shocks – jolts that weren't sufficient to be harmful, but that were powerful enough to make limbs twitch – and partici- pants were asked to rank their subjective experience of the pain. Some then received three twenty-minute lessons in mindfulness meditation over the course of the next few days, showing them how to develop non-judgmental awareness of their thoughts, emotions, and sensations. When further electric shocks were administered, those who used the meditation techniques reported significantly reduced pain. (In a related experiment by Zeidan's team, using brain scans and pain created by a hot plate, meditation appeared to lead to less pain for every participant, with the reductions ranging from 11 to 93 per cent.) A critic might counter that the meditation was merely providing a distraction, giving the participants something else to focus on – so Zeidan had another group perform a mathematics task while being shocked. Distraction did have some effect, but it was nowhere near as large as that of meditation. And the meditation lessons, unlike distraction, lowered pain levels even when participants didn't actively meditate during the shocks.

'It was kind of freaky for me,' Zeidan said. 'I was ramping at four to five hundred milliamps, and their arms would be jolting back and forth, because the current was stimulating a motor nerve.' Yet still their pain assessments remained low. Meditation, Zeidan believes, 'had taught them that distractions, feelings and emotions are momentary, [and] don't require a label or judgment, because the moment is already over. With the meditation training, they would acknowledge the pain, they realise what it is, but they let it go. They learn to bring their attention back to the present.' If you've ever gripped the arms of a dentist's chair, in expectation of imminent agony that never actually arrives, you'll know that a big part of the problem is attachment to thoughts about pain, the fear of its arrival, and the internal struggle to avoid it. In Zeidan's laboratory, focusing non-attachedly on the experience of pain itself rendered the experience much less distressing.

As the hours turned into days at the Insight Meditation Society, however, my attachments seemed only to grow more intractable. By the second day, the song lyrics had faded, but in their place came darker irritations. Gradually, I started to become aware of a young man sitting just behind me and to the left. I had noticed him when he first entered the meditation hall, and had felt a flash of annoyance at the time: something about him, especially his beard, had struck me as too calculatedly dishevelled, as if he were trying to make a statement. Now his audible breathing was starting to irritate me, too. It seemed studied, unnatural, somehow theatrical. My irritation slowly intensified – a reaction that struck me as entirely reasonable and proportionate at the time. It was all beginning to feel like a personal attack. How much contempt must the bearded meditator have for me, I seethed silently, deliberately to decide to ruin the serenity of my meditation by behaving so obnoxiously?

Experienced retreat-goers, it turns out, have a term for this phenomenon. They call it a 'vipassana vendetta'. In the stillness, tiny irritations become magnified into full-blown hate campaigns; the mind is so conditioned to attaching to storylines that it seizes upon whatever's available. Being on retreat had temporarily separated me from all the real causes of distress in my life, and so, apparently, I was inventing new ones. As I shuffled to my narrow bed that evening, I was still smarting about the loud-breathing man. I did let go of the vendetta eventually – but only because I'd fallen into an exhausted and dreamless sleep.

One of the most obvious objections to non-attachment as a way of life is that it seems so passive. Granted, it might be a way of becoming more chilled out, but wouldn't it mean never getting anything done? The Buddhist monk spending decades in meditation might be at one with the universe, but it's not clear that the rest of us should want to emulate him. Attachment, this argument runs, is the only thing that motivates anyone to accomplish anything worthwhile in the first place. If you weren't attached to things being a certain way, rather than another way – and to feeling certain emotions, rather than others – why would you ever attempt to thrive professionally, to better your material circumstances, to raise children, or to change the world? There's a persuasive retort to this, though. Just as the Stoic notion of acceptance need not entail resignation, Buddhist non-attachment can be a rigorously practical way of accomplishing worthwhile activities. To understand why, consider the most ubiquitous and frustrating barrier to getting things done: the near-universal curse of procrastination.

You are probably already much too familiar with the truth that most anti-procrastination advice just doesn't work, or at least not for very long. Motivational books, tapes and seminars might leave you feeling briefly excited, but that feeling soon fades. Ambitious lists of goals and systems of rewards seem like a great idea when you construct them, but feel stale the next morning; inspiring mottos on posters and coffee mugs swiftly lose their ability to inspire. Procrastination sets in again, sometimes deeper than before. Which is, a cynic might suggest, how motivational speakers and self-help authors guarantee themselves a reliable income: if their products delivered lasting change, they would have much less repeat custom.

The problem with all these motivational tips and tricks is that they aren't really about 'how to get things done' at all. They're about how to feel in the mood for getting things done. 'If we get the right emotion, we can get ourselves to do *anything*!' says Tony Robbins, author of *Awaken the Giant Within*, whose books and speeches

fixate on this theme. (At Robbins's motivational seminars, participants are invited to pump themselves up by walking barefoot across
hot coals.) As we've seen, though, the ideas that self-help gurus
express so hyperbolically are often only extreme versions of how
the rest of us think. The most common response to procrastination
is indeed to try to 'get the right emotion': to try to motivate yourself to feel like getting on with the job.

The problem is that *feeling like* acting and *actually* acting are
two different things. A person mired deep in procrastination
might claim he is unable to work, but what he really means is
that he is unable to make himself feel like working. The author
Julie Fast, who writes about the psychology of depression, points
out that even when a person is so depressed that she is unable
to get out of bed in the morning – something Fast has experienced
for herself – it's more accurate to say that she's unable to *feel like*
getting out of bed. This isn't meant to imply that procrastinators,
or the severely depressed, should simply pull their socks up and
get over it. Rather, it highlights the way that we tend to confuse
acting with feeling like acting, and how most motivational techniques are really designed to change how you *feel*. They're built,
in other words, on a form of attachment – on strengthening your
investment in a specific kind of emotion.

Sometimes that can help. But sometimes you simply can't
make yourself feel like acting. And in those situations, motivational advice risks making things worse, by surreptitiously
strengthening your belief that you need to feel motivated before
you can act. By encouraging an attachment to a particular
emotional state, it actually inserts an additional hurdle between
you and your goal. The subtext is that if you can't make yourself
feel excited and pleased about getting down to work, then you
can't get down to work.

Taking a non-attached stance towards procrastination, by contrast, starts from a different question: Who says you need to wait until you 'feel like' doing something in order to start doing it? The problem, from this perspective, isn't that you don't feel motivated; it's that you imagine you need to feel motivated. If you can regard your thoughts and emotions about whatever you're procrastinating on as passing weather, you'll realise that your reluctance about working isn't something that needs to be eradicated or transformed into positivity. You can coexist with it. You can note the procrastinatory feelings and act anyway.

It is illuminating to note, here, how the daily rituals and working routines of prolific authors and artists – people who really do get a lot done – very rarely include techniques for 'getting motivated' or 'feeling inspired'. Quite the opposite: they tend to emphasise the mechanics of the working process, focusing not on generating the right mood, but on accomplishing certain physical actions, regardless of mood. Anthony Trollope wrote for three hours each morning before leaving to go to his job as an executive at the post office; if he finished a novel within a three-hour period, he simply moved on to the next. (He wrote forty-seven novels over the course of his life.) The routines of almost all famous writers, from Charles Darwin to John Grisham, similarly emphasise specific starting times, or number of hours worked, or words written. Such rituals provide a structure to work in, whether or not the feeling of motivation or inspiration happens to be present. They let people work alongside negative or positive emotions, instead of getting distracted by the effort of cultivating only positive ones. 'Inspiration is for amateurs,' the artist Chuck Close once memorably observed. 'The rest of us just show up and get to work.'

No approach to psychology better expresses the pragmatic

benefits of non-attachment than Morita Therapy, the school founded by the early twentieth-century Japanese psychologist Shoma Morita. The head of psychiatry at Jikei University School of Medicine in Tokyo, Morita was heavily influenced by Buddhism, and especially its perspective on thoughts and emotions as mental weather – as things that happen to us, and with which we can coexist in peace. 'People . . . think that they should always like what they do, and that their lives should be trouble-free,' Morita wrote. 'Consequently, their mental energy is wasted by their impossible attempts to avoid feelings of displeasure or boredom.'

One contemporary practitioner of Morita Therapy, James Hill, expresses this distinctive approach as follows: 'Many western therapeutic methods focus on trying to successfully manage or modify our feeling-states. The underlying assumption is that if our feelings can be altered [or] reduced, we will be more able to live meaningful and effective lives; that it is our feelings that hold us back . . . [But] is it accurate to assume that we must "overcome" fear to jump off the high dive at the pool, or increase our confidence before we ask someone out on a date? If it was, most of us would still be waiting to do these things. Our life experience teaches that it is not necessary to change our feelings in order to take action . . . Once we learn to accept our feelings, we find that we can take action without changing our feeling-states.' We can feel the fear and do it anyway.

By the end of the fourth day at the Insight Meditation Society, things were much improved. The bearded man's breathing had ceased to annoy. All of us seemed to have settled into the timetable that governed our waking, sleeping, meditating and eating; where before it had felt rigid and militaristic, now it cradled us through the day. I was actually starting to enjoy meditating – even the walking meditation, which involved moving at a glacial pace across the meditation hall, trying to divide the sensations of each footstep into the component parts of 'lifting', 'moving' and 'placing', and which I had initially concluded was a waste of time. When, during occasional breaks, I managed to sneak out onto the forest paths behind the meditation centre, I found I had become hyper-attuned to my environment; every crackle of every twig underfoot registered like a splintering diamond. Meanwhile, the vegetarian food we were served in the dining room – nondescript lentil stews, peanut butter on rye crackers, that sort of thing – had started to taste extraordinary. I discovered subtle sub-flavours in peanut butter I'd never have imagined might be hiding there. The Massachusetts winter sunset, viewed from the building's main porch, was often so beautiful as to be almost painful. At night, I was sleeping more deeply than I could remember.

And then it all went wrong. Without my noticing the precise moment of transition, the silence of the meditation hall became a combination of courtroom and torture chamber. For hours, I was attacked by barrages of negative thoughts and their associated emotions – anxious ones, guilty ones, worried ones, hostile, bored, impatient and even terrified ones – as if they had all been gathering, just out of sight, for years, waiting for this moment to pounce. Above all, they were self-critical. I was suddenly aware – and somehow all at once – of countless occasions in my life on which I had behaved badly towards other people: my parents, my sister, friends, girlfriends, or colleagues. Many of these infractions were relatively small in the scheme of things – harsh words spoken, relationships insufficiently nurtured – but they filled me with sorrow. Months afterwards, I would encounter Buddhist writings suggesting that this was a well-recognised early step on the 'progress of insight', the stages through which a meditator is traditionally held to pass: it was called 'knowledge of cause and effect', and had to do with perceiving afresh how one's actions always had consequences. The sorrow that accompanied these realisations, from a Buddhist point of view, is a good thing; it is the fertile soil in which compassion can take root.

After about a day of this, though, I began to notice something. The situation in my mind was far from quiet or relaxed. And yet my constant efforts to return to focusing on my breath – to avoid becoming attached to thoughts or emotions – seemed to be having an effect. My vantage point on my mental activity had altered subtly, as if I'd climbed two rungs up a stepladder in order to observe it from above. I was less enmeshed in it all. As Shoma Morita might have put it, I was beginning to see it all as mere mental events, to be non-judgmentally noticed. Much of my thinking concerned the past or the future, but I was no longer being yanked off into daydreams or unpleasant memories; I was absolutely present, there on the cushion, watching the performance with something less like panic and more like interest. In some monasteries in the Zen tradition, a monk is charged with creeping up behind his fellow monks and hitting them with a thin wooden stick, or *keisaku*, in order to snap them into exactly this kind of utter presence. They didn't hit people with sticks at the Insight Meditation Society, but I felt like someone had. I was watching my own mind with total alertness.

The strangest part, though, and the part that is hardest to put into words, was the question of where I was watching all this *from*. If I'd stepped away from being enmeshed in my thoughts, where was this point of observation? Nowhere? Everywhere? I felt as if I had stepped into a void. I recalled my conversation with Adina in the taxi, and Pema Chödrön's advice about 'relaxing into the groundlessness of our situation'. It was suddenly apparent to me that I spent my regular life in a state of desperate clinging to thinking, to trying to avoid falling into the void that lay behind thoughts. Except now I was in the void, and it wasn't terrifying at all. By the time the retreat drew to a close, I found to my surprise that I didn't want it to end; I could easily have stayed another week. Moreover, I felt as if I were among friends. Even though I had never exchanged words with most of the other retreatants – and wouldn't have recognised them in the street, given that we'd been keeping our eyes downcast – a tangible sense of community had arisen in the meditation hall. When the gong rang to indicate that we could speak again, small talk felt scratchy and awkward; it seemed to interfere with the companionship.

'Well, that was . . . ' said Adina, trailing into silence when I encountered her on the porch as we made our preparations to leave. Encapsulating the week in a few words seemed futile.

'I know what you mean,' I replied.

By the time I made it onto the train back to New York, I had a throbbing headache: the normal noises of the non-meditating world were too much for my silence-adapted mind. Discovering the number of emails waiting in my inbox didn't help. But the stressed-out thoughts did slide away more swiftly than before. It seemed I could live with a little bad weather.

All this is only one small part of Buddhism's radical perspective on psychology. But the point is central to any 'negative' approach to happiness: it is rarely wise to struggle to change the weather. 'Clear mind is like the full moon in the sky,' Seung Sahn, a Korean Zen master of the old school, who carried a hitting stick, told one audience in America in the 1970s. 'Sometimes clouds come and cover it, but the moon is always behind them. Clouds go away, then the moon shines brightly. So don't worry about clear mind; it is always there. When thinking comes, behind it is clear mind. When thinking goes, there is only clear mind. Thinking comes and goes, comes and goes. You must not be attached to the coming and going.' And if that wasn't sufficient to jolt his listeners into the realisation that they did not need to be attached to their mental storylines, that they could choose to observe their thoughts and feelings non-judgmentally, and thus find peace behind the pandemonium? 'Then,' Seung Sahn was fond of saying, 'I hit you thirty times with my stick!'

4

Goal Crazy

When Trying to Control the Future Doesn't Work

Future, *n.* That period of time in which our affairs prosper,
our friends are true and our happiness is assured.

— Ambrose Bierce, *The Devil's Dictionary*

IN 1996, A TWENTY-EIGHT-YEAR-OLD from Indiana named
Christopher Kayes signed up with an adventure travel company
to go trekking in the Himalayas. His intention, though it would
prove ironic in hindsight, was to take a relaxing break. A punishing
career as a stockbroker, and then as a corporate consultant, had
left him burned out. Kayes had always been interested in the
psychology of the business world, and so he had decided to pursue
a doctorate in organisational behaviour instead. But first he needed
time off, and when he saw an advertisement in a travel magazine
for a group hiking expedition to Nepal, it seemed like the perfect
answer. As the plane descended into Kathmandu, he recalled later,
he was looking forward to 'a refreshing immersion in Nepalese
culture', surrounded by the beauty of the Himalayas. But what
Kayes encountered in the mountains was a troubling psychological
puzzle that was to dominate his life for years to come.

While Kayes and his fellow hikers were exploring the foothills of Mount Everest, camping at night in tents, a disaster of historical proportions was unfolding near the mountain's peak. Fifteen climbers died on Everest during that year's climbing season, eight of them during a single twenty-four-hour period that has since entered mountaineering lore, thanks largely to the bestselling book *Into Thin Air*, by the climber and journalist Jon Krakauer, who was among those on the mountain at the time. Kayes himself encountered some of the climbers and rescue workers who had been involved – exhausted men, emerging dazed into the foothills, struggling to make sense of what had happened.

Even in the modern era of commercial Everest expeditions, when anyone with sufficient money and some climbing skills can pay to be escorted to the summit, it's still not that unusual for people to die in the attempt. What made the 1996 disaster so chilling – apart from the sheer number of dead – was the fact that it seemed uniquely inexplicable. The weather on the peak was not more perilous than usual. There were no sudden avalanches during the period when most of the climbers perished. The paying customers were all sufficiently skilled for the undertaking. *Into Thin Air*, controversially, attributed the tragedy in part to the stubbornness and arrogance of Anatoli Boukreev, a Kazakhstani climbing guide. There is some evidence for this, but it is ultimately dissatisfying as an explanation, too. Mountaineers, as a group, tend towards stubbornness and arrogance. Yet disasters on the scale of Everest in 1996 are mercifully rare.

In the end, what happened that year looked more like an outbreak of mass irrationality – an episode that reached its apogee around noon on 10 May at the Hillary Step, a wall of rock just 720 feet from the summit, in an event that has since become known as 'the traffic jam'. Teams from New Zealand, the United

States and Taiwan – thirty-four climbers in total – were all attempting the final stage of the ascent that day, from Camp Four, at 26,000 feet, to the summit, at 29,000 feet. The Americans and New Zealanders had co-ordinated their efforts, so as to ensure a smooth progression up and down the mountain. But the Taiwanese climbers were reneging on an agreement not to climb the same day, and an advance team of guides had failed to secure safety ropes at the Hillary Step according to plan, with the result that the smooth progression soon turned into a bottleneck.

Timing is one of the most important variables in any assault on Everest, and so climbers generally observe strict 'turnaround times'. Leaving Camp Four at midnight, a climber can hope to reach the summit by midday, or soon after. But if he or she fails to make it there by the pre-arranged turnaround time – which might be anywhere from noon until two in the afternoon, depending on weather conditions, and the team leader's attitude to risk – it becomes essential to call off the attempt and turn back. Failure to do so means the climber risks running out of bottled oxygen and facing Everest's most dangerous weather in the dark. Yet confronted with the traffic jam at the Hillary Step, the teams pushed on, disregarding their turnaround times. Back at Camp Four, the American mountaineer Ed Viesturs watched the climbers' slow progress through a telescope, and found it hard to believe what he was seeing. 'They've already been climbing for hours, and they still aren't on the summit,' he remembered thinking to himself, with rising alarm. 'Why haven't they turned around?'

Members of all three teams continued arriving at the summit for two hours after two o'clock, the latest safe turnaround time. Doug Hansen, a postal service worker from Washington state who was a paying client of the New Zealand group, was the last to do

so, at the astonishingly late time of just after four o'clock. He had
ascended Everest the year before, but had been forced to turn
back a few hundred feet from the top. This time, he never made
it back down. Like seven others, he was caught in intense blizzards
as darkness fell, which made navigation of the mountain impossible, and sent temperatures plunging to −40°F. They lay dying,
unreached by the frantic rescue attempts that saved several other
climbers' lives. Years after climbing Everest had become a feasible
project for amateurs as well as professionals, 1996 saw the highest
recorded death toll in the mountain's history. And even today,
nobody clearly understands why.

Except, just possibly, Chris Kayes. A former stockbroker turned
expert on organisational behaviour might seem to have little to
contribute to the post-mortem of a mountaineering disaster. But
the more Kayes learned of what had happened, and as he
continued to follow the case after returning home, the more it
reminded him of a phenomenon he had witnessed all too
frequently among businesspeople. The Everest climbers, Kayes
suspected, had been 'lured into destruction by their passion for
goals'. His hypothesis was that the more they fixated on the
endpoint – a successful summiting of the mountain – the more
that goal became not just an external target but a part of their
own identities, of their senses of themselves as accomplished
guides or high-achieving amateurs. If his hunch about the
climbers was right, it would have become progressively more
difficult for them to sacrifice their goal, despite accumulating
evidence that it was becoming a suicidal one. Indeed, that accumulating evidence, Kayes was convinced, would have *hardened* the
climbers' determination not to turn back. The climb would have
become a struggle not merely to reach the summit, but to preserve
their sense of identity. In theology, the term 'theodicy' refers to

the effort to maintain belief in a benevolent god, despite the prevalence of evil in the world; the phrase is occasionally used to describe the effort to maintain any belief in the face of contradictory evidence. Borrowing that language, Chris Kayes termed the syndrome he had identified 'goalodicy'.

During his years in the corporate world, Kayes had been troubled to watch goalsetting achieve the status of religious dogma among his colleagues. The situation hasn't changed much today. The hallmark of a visionary leader, it is widely held, is the willingness to set big, audacious goals for his or her organisation, and then to focus every resource on achieving them. Individual employees, meanwhile, are encouraged, and sometimes obliged, to define their own personal work objectives, frequently in the form of 'SMART' goals. (The acronym stands for 'specific, measurable, attainable, realistic, and time-bounded'.) Numerous self-help books advocate ambitious and highly specific goals as the master key to a successful and satisfying life: 'By this time next year, I will be married to the woman of my dreams/sitting on the balcony of my beach house/earning £10,000 per month!' One of the practice's most passionate evangelists, Brian Tracy, in his book *Goals! How to Get Everything You Want – Faster Than You Ever Thought Possible*, insists that 'Living without clear goals is like driving in a thick fog . . . Clear goals enable you to step on the accelerator of your own life, and race ahead rapidly.'

Yet Kayes couldn't help but notice that it frequently didn't work out that way. A business goal would be set, announced, and generally greeted with enthusiasm. But then evidence would begin to emerge that it had been an unwise one – and goalodicy would kick in as a response. The negative evidence would be reinterpreted as a reason to invest *more* effort and resources in pursuit of the goal. And so things would, not surprisingly, go even more wrong. Kayes believed that a similar thing had happened on Everest in 1996.

Chris Kayes is now a professor of management science at George Washington University in Washington, DC, and as he has travelled the lecture circuit in recent years, using Everest as a metaphor for all that is wrong with our obsession with goals, he has frequently found himself giving offence. 'A businessperson should not study topics filled with such great tragedy and emotion,' one Russian student lectured him curtly by email. 'Questions of tragedy and the dilemmas of human existence should be left to the poet, the novelist, and the playwright. These topics have nothing to do with why we study leadership in organisations.' But Kayes couldn't let it drop. 'It would be accurate to say that I think about the Everest disaster probably every day,' he told me. 'Almost like it was a death in my own family. "Haunted" would definitely be the right word.' And there is persuasive evidence for Kayes's hypothesis about what happened on the mountain, hidden away in a largely forgotten psychology study that was conducted in 1963. The study's participants were professional mountaineers, undertaking an expedition to Everest.

That year, seventeen climbers were attempting to become the first Americans to reach the summit, and a psychologist named James Lester realised that the expedition presented an ideal opportunity to investigate what drove people to attempt such ambitious and dangerous feats. With funding provided by the United States Navy, Lester and a handful of colleagues gathered the mountaineers in Berkeley, California, where they administered a series of personality tests. Then – demonstrating an unusual degree of commitment to his research – Lester left sunny California for Mount Everest, accompanying the climbers as far as Camp Two, at 21,000 feet. There, he administered further tests on the climbers and their Sherpa guides. In his book *Destructive Goal Pursuit: The Mount Everest Disaster*, Chris Kayes relates Lester's basic finding about the typical Everest climber: he was someone who demonstrated 'considerable restlessness, dislike for routine, desire for autonomy, tendency to be dominant in personal relations, and a lack of interest in social interaction for its own sake. Their felt need for achievement and independence was very high.' No surprises there: Lester had confirmed the truism that climbers tend to be domineering loners with little regard for social convention. But more intriguing findings were to emerge from the daily diaries that Lester asked the climbers to keep for the duration of the three-month period they spent preparing for, then carrying out, their trek to the mountain's summit.

En route to base camp, the American team had split into two dissenting groups, each with a very different idea of how best to reach the top. The larger group favoured the well-established route via the South Col, a mountain pass ravaged by high winds, leaving it relatively free of snow. But a smaller group wanted to approach via the remote and never previously attempted West Ridge. (Even today, in a morbid statistical oddity, the fatality rate for the West Ridge is higher than 100 per cent, meaning that more people have died there than have reached the summit that way.) Noting the difference of opinion among the climbers, Lester made sure that their diaries included regular updates on how optimistic or pessimistic they were feeling about their chosen route.

Subsequent analysis of the diaries revealed an unexpected pattern. As the day of the summit attempt neared, the West Ridge group's optimism began to fade rapidly, replaced by a gnawing sense of uncertainty. That was only to be expected, given that their route was untried. But as the climbers' uncertainty and pessimism about the West Ridge option increased, the diaries

revealed, so did their commitment to it. 'The more uncertain
climbers felt about their possible success in reaching the summit,'
as Kayes puts it, 'the more likely they were to invest in their
particular strategy.' A bizarre and self-reinforcing loop took hold:
team members would actively seek out negative information
about their goal – looking for evidence of weather patterns, for
example, that might render the West Ridge approach even more
risky than usual – which would increase their feelings of uncertainty. But then, in an effort to extinguish that uncertainty, the
climbers would increase their emotional investment in their
decision. The goal, it seemed, had become a part of their identity,
and so their uncertainty about the goal no longer merely threatened the plan; it threatened them as individuals. They were so
eager to eliminate these feelings of uncertainty that they clung
ever harder to a clear, firm and specific plan that provided them
with a sense of certainty about the future – even though that plan
was looking increasingly reckless. They were firmly in the grip of
goalodicy.

The happy conclusion of the 1963 expedition – much as it
spoils the neatness of Kayes's argument – is that the West Ridge
climbers went ahead with their dangerous plan, and survived.
Too many of the relevant participants in the 1996 drama perished,
meanwhile, for us ever to know with confidence exactly how
far the same thought processes were to blame. But Beck Weathers,
a paying client that year who was twice left for dead on the
mountain – he lost his nose and several fingers to frostbite,
having dragged himself back to camp – testified to the plausibility
of the notion. 'You can overpursue goals,' he reflected afterwards.
'You can become obsessed with goals.'

Mountaineers, of course, do not speak in the corporate
language of targets and goalsetting. But when they refer to

'summit fever' – that strange, sometimes fatal magnetism that certain peaks seem to exert upon the minds of climbers – they are intuitively identifying something similar: a commitment to a goal that, like sirens luring sailors onto the rocks, destroys those who struggle too hard to achieve it. Ed Viesturs, who watched the 1996 tragedy through his telescope, spoke of this lure in vivid terms. 'When you're up there, you've spent years of training, months of preparation, and weeks of climbing, and you're within view of the summit, and you know, you have – in the back of your mind, you're telling yourself "We should turn around, 'cause we're late, we're gonna run out of oxygen . . . " But you see the summit, and it draws you there. And a lot of people – it's so magnetic that they tend to break their rules, and they go to the summit. And on a good day, you can get away with it. And on a bad day, you'll die.'

If you've ever read a popular book about the importance of planning for the future, you will almost certainly have encountered a reference – and quite possibly several – to the Yale Study of Goals. This is a now-legendary finding about the importance of creating detailed plans for your life: it is cited in the aforementioned *Goals!*, by Brian Tracy, but also in scores of other works, from the supposedly scholarly (books with titles such as *Psychological Foundations of Success*) to the more streetwise (the management manual *Train Your People and Whack the Competition*). The essentials of the study are as follows: in 1953, students graduating from Yale University were asked by researchers whether or not they had formulated specific, written-down goals for the rest of their lives. Only 3 per cent of them said they had. Two decades later, the researchers tracked down the class of '53, to see how their lives

had turned out. The results were unequivocal: the 3 per cent of
graduates with written goals had amassed greater financial wealth
than the other 97 per cent combined. It is a jaw-dropping finding,
and a powerful lesson to any young person thinking of just drifting
through life. It isn't surprising, then, that it achieved the status of
legend in the world of self-help, and in many corners of corporate
life. The only problem is that it is indeed a legend: the Yale Study
of Goals never took place.

Some years ago, a journalist from the technology magazine
Fast Company set out to trace the source of the alleged study. No
academic journal reference was ever cited when it was mentioned,
so he began by asking the motivational gurus who liked to quote
it. Disconcertingly, when asked for their sources, they pointed at
each other. Tony Robbins suggested asking Brian Tracy, who in
turn suggested Zig Ziglar, a veteran of the motivational-speaker
circuit, and a regular fixture at Get Motivated! seminars.
Completing the circle, Zig Ziglar recommended asking Tony
Robbins.

Taking matters into my own hands, I called a senior Yale
University archivist, Beverly Waters. She seemed friendly and eager
to help, but when I mentioned the goals study, a note of frustration
entered her voice. 'I did a systematic check, years ago, when this
first arose, and there was nothing,' she said. 'Then the secretary
of the graduating class of 1953 did another systematic check, and
nobody he spoke to had ever been asked to fill out such a questionnaire, or anything like that.' She added that it was highly
unlikely that it had happened in some other year, and been
wrongly described as taking place in 1953, because the Association
of Yale Alumni would have been involved – and nobody there
could trace anyone who remembered it. Waters sighed. 'It's just
too good not to be true, I guess,' she said.

Of course, the non-existence of one study about the benefits of setting goals does not disprove the suggestion that setting goals has benefits; there is plenty of very real research testifying to the fact that the practice can be useful. What the story indicates, instead, is how far the fascination with goals has gone. You might never have written down any 'life goals' yourself, and you might well disagree with the imaginary Yale study's implication that material wealth is the ticket to happiness. But the basic urge beneath all this is nearly universal. At some point in your life, and perhaps at many points, you likely have decided upon some goal – to find a spouse, to get a specific kind of job, to live in a particular town – and then devised a plan to attain it. Interpreted sufficiently broadly, setting goals and carrying out plans to achieve them is how many of us spend most of our waking hours. Whether or not we use the word 'goals', we're forever making plans based upon desired outcomes. 'Consider any individual at any period of his life,' wrote the great French political philosopher Alexis de Tocqueville, 'and you will always find him preoccupied with fresh plans to increase his comfort.' Tocqueville's use of the word 'comfort' should not distract us here; we are, of course, capable of setting far grander and more selfless goals than that. But the deeper truth remains: many of us are perpetually preoccupied with plans.

It is precisely this preoccupation that the followers of the 'negative path' to happiness call into question – because it turns out that setting and then chasing after goals can often backfire in horrible ways. There is a good case to be made that many of us, and many of the organisations for which we work, would do better to spend less time on goalsetting, and, more generally, to focus with less intensity on planning for how we would like the future to turn out.

At the core of this outlook is the insight that Chris Kayes and James Lester both reached in their studies of Everest mountaineers: that what motivates our investment in goals and planning for the future, much of the time, isn't any sober recognition of the virtues of preparation and looking ahead. Rather, it's something much more emotional: how deeply uncomfortable we are made by feelings of uncertainty. Faced with the anxiety of not knowing what the future holds, we invest ever more fiercely in our preferred vision of that future – not because it will help us achieve it, but because it helps rid us of feelings of uncertainty in the present. 'Uncertainty prompts us to idealise the future,' Kayes told me. 'We tell ourselves that everything will be OK, just as long as I can reach this projection of the future.' Obviously, climbing Mount Everest requires plenty of planning and implies a specific goal – reaching the summit. But to Kayes, the evidence suggested that in 1996, an aversion to feelings of uncertainty might have tipped the balance in favour of a fatal overinvestment in goals.

We fear the feeling of uncertainty to an extraordinary degree – the psychologist Dorothy Rowe argues that we fear it more than death itself – and we will go to extraordinary lengths, even fatal ones, to get rid of it. As we will see later in this chapter, though, there is a powerful alternative possibility: we could learn to become more comfortable with uncertainty, and to exploit the potential hidden within it, both to feel better in the present and to achieve more success in the future.

It is alarming to consider how many major life decisions we take primarily in order to minimise present-moment emotional discomfort. Try the following potentially mortifying exercise in self-examination. Consider any significant decision you've ever taken that you subsequently came to regret: a relationship you entered despite being dimly aware that it wasn't for you, or a job you accepted even though, looking back, it's clear that it was mismatched to your interests or abilities. If it felt like a difficult decision at the time, then it's likely that, prior to taking it, you felt the gut-knotting ache of uncertainty; afterwards, having made a decision, did those feelings subside? If so, this points to the troubling possibility that your primary motivation in taking the decision wasn't any rational consideration of its rightness for you, but simply the urgent need to get rid of your feelings of uncertainty. Here are the words of one blogger on psychology, David Cain, reflecting on how an intolerance for uncertainty once dominated his own choices: 'It's quite disturbing to take a mental inventory of where [the intolerance for uncertainty] has steered my life,' he writes. 'It's the reason I spent three years and ten thousand dollars learning computer programming, when I didn't really want to do it for a living. It's the reason behind every single day I've spent working on careers that don't inspire me. [Uncertainty] feels like you're sinking, and [that] it is positively imperative to scramble to the next patch of firm ground, whatever direction it may be in. Once you get there, you can let yourself breathe.' Clinging too tightly to goals is one of the principal ways in which we express the obsession with reaching that next patch of ground.

To understand one of the many reasons why goals can backfire, consider the experience of trying to hail a taxi in a major city during a rainstorm. If you've ever had to do this, you'll be familiar with the despair it can induce – and you probably think you understand why it's so difficult, since it seems like the kind of economics problem even a five-year-old could solve. When it rains, more people want cabs, and so demand outstrips supply, making it harder to find an empty vehicle. That's obvious, surely? So when the economist Colin Camerer and three of his colleagues

set out to investigate the problem of the rainy-day taxi shortage
– taking New York City as their field of study – you can imagine
the kind of looks they might have received from their colleagues.

Except, as their research revealed, the reason for the problem
isn't as obvious as it appears. Demand for taxis does surge when
it rains. But something much stranger happens at the same time:
the supply of taxis shrinks. This contradicts the standard economic
assumption that when people stand to earn more money, they
work more. You might have expected cab drivers, who have some
discretion over the hours they work, to work the most when
demand was highest. Instead, they clocked off *earlier* when it
rained.

Further investigation revealed that the culprit was goals. New
York taxi drivers rent their vehicles in twelve-hour shifts, and
commonly set themselves the daily goal of taking in double the
amount of money that it costs to rent the cab. When it rains, they
meet their goal more rapidly and head home sooner. New Yorkers
are thus deprived of taxis during exactly the weather conditions
in which they need them most, while drivers are deprived of
additional income at exactly the time when it would be easiest
to earn.

The point is not that it's wrong for a taxi driver to choose
more leisure time over more income, of course – that's an entirely
defensible choice – but that it makes no sense to take that time
off when it's raining. Far from behaving like stereotypically
rational economic actors, the drivers appeared to act more like
the pigeons in experiments conducted by the behaviourist
psychologist B. F. Skinner. Having learned to obtain a food pellet
by pecking on a mechanism in its cage, Skinner observed, a pigeon
would indulge in a 'post-pellet pause', relaxing after having
attained a predetermined goal.

A taxi driver's daily income goal is a very different matter to the goal of climbing Everest, and the researchers did not investigate the drivers' emotional motivations. But it is possible to see the taxi-shortage problem as another, more minor example of how uncomfortable we're made by uncertainty. The drivers, it would appear, preferred the regularity and reliability of a predictable daily income to the uncertainty of remaining open to the possibility of earning more. They had invested in their goals beyond the point that doing so served their best interests.

New York cab drivers were much on the mind of a university professor named Lisa Ordóñez when, in 2009, she and three of her colleagues embarked upon the heretical project of questioning goalsetting. In their academic field, management studies, the wisdom of goalsetting was rarely questioned, thanks largely to the work of two North American management theorists, Gary Latham and Edwin Locke. Over the course of the previous four decades, Latham and Locke had established themselves as the godfathers of goalsetting, publishing more than twenty books between them. Their credo was one of the very first things taught to incoming students at business schools: to be a success as an entrepreneur, what you needed first was a business plan, focused on specific goals. Anything less was unacceptable. 'When people are asked to do their best, they don't,' Edwin Locke told one interviewer. 'It's too vague.'

Ordóñez and her colleagues mounted the case for the opposition in a 2009 paper with a heavy-handed pun for its title – 'Goals Gone Wild' – in the usually rather dry pages of the journal *Academy of Management Perspectives*. The goalsetting that worked so well in Latham and Locke's studies, they pointed out, had various nasty side effects in their own experiments. For example: clearly defined goals seemed to motivate people to cheat. In one such study, participants were given the task of making words from a set of random letters, as in Scrabble; the experiment gave them opportunities to report their progress anonymously. Those given a target to reach lied far more frequently than did those instructed merely to 'do your best'. More important, though, Ordóñez and her fellow heretics argued, goalsetting worked vastly less well outside the psychology lab settings in which such studies took place. In real life, an obsession with goals seemed far more often to land people and organisations in trouble.

One illuminating example of the problem concerns the American automobile behemoth General Motors. The turn of the millennium found GM in a serious predicament, losing customers and profits to more nimble, primarily Japanese, competitors. Following Latham and Locke's philosophy to the letter, executives at GM's headquarters in Detroit came up with a goal, crystallised in a number: twenty-nine. Twenty-nine, the company announced amid much media fanfare, was the percentage of the American car market that it would recapture, reasserting its old dominance. Twenty-nine was also the number displayed upon small gold lapel pins, worn by senior figures at GM to demonstrate their commitment to the plan. At corporate gatherings, and in internal GM documents, twenty-nine was the target drummed into everyone from salespeople to engineers to public-relations officers.

Yet the plan not only failed to work – it made things worse. Obsessed with winning back market share, GM spent its dwindling finances on money-off schemes and clever advertising, trying to lure drivers into purchasing its unpopular cars, rather than investing in the more speculative and open-ended – and thus more uncertain – research that might have resulted in more innovative and more popular vehicles. There were certainly many other reasons for GM's ongoing decline. But twenty-nine became a fetish, distorting the organisation in damaging ways, fuelling short-termism and blinkered vision, all so that the numbers in the business news headlines might match those on the vice-presidents' lapels. But that never happened. GM continued spiralling towards failure, and went bankrupt in 2009; it ended up taking a bailout from Washington. At the Detroit Auto Show of 2010, the firm's newly installed president for North America, keen to show how much GM had changed, used the twenty-nine campaign as an example of what it would no longer be doing. 'We're not printing [lapel] pins,' he told a radio reporter. 'We're not doing any of that stuff.'

It is safe to say that Edwin Locke and Gary Latham's response to 'Goals Gone Wild' was among the more furious outbursts ever to have been published in *Academy of Management Perspectives*. Ordóñez and her colleagues were accused of being extremists, of using 'scare tactics', of abandoning good scholarship by stringing together anecdotes, of 'spreading falsehoods and insults', and of 'making unverified assertions'. 'Oh, my God!', Ordóñez exclaimed, when I asked her about the dispute. 'My face was hot for a week. It was just so completely personal. But put yourself in their shoes. They had spent forty years doing research into how wonderful goals can be, and here we were, coming and pointing out the pitfalls. It was nothing but a temper tantrum.'

The reason all this academic infighting matters to anyone else is that the two sides represent two fundamentally different ways of thinking about planning for the future. It was unfair, as it happened, for Locke and Latham to imply that Ordóñez and her colleagues had ignored experimental data altogether in favour of anecdotes. But the real lesson of 'Goals Gone Wild' is that the simplified conditions of the laboratory almost never apply in real

life. In most artificial studies of goalsetting, participants are faced
with a single task or simple set of tasks, such as the word game
mentioned earlier; some of them are then encouraged to approach
the task with a goal firmly in mind, while others are not. But as
the case of GM suggests, outside the laboratory – whether in
business, or in life in general – no situation is ever anywhere close
to being this simple. In singling out one goal, or set of goals, and
striving to meet it, you will invariably exert an effect on other,
interlinked aspects of the thing you're trying to change. In an
automobile manufacturing company, that might mean starving
your research division of funding in an effort to meet a predetermined market share. Applied to the personal realm, it might
mean attaining your goals at the expense of ruining your life.
During one course he taught, Chris Kayes recalled, 'an executive
came up to me at the end of a session and told me his goal had
been to become a millionaire by the age of forty. That's something
you hear all the time in business schools. And he'd done it – he
was forty-two, so he was right on target. But he was also divorced
and had health problems. And his kids didn't talk to him anymore.'
Another student had been furiously training for a marathon when
he first met her. She succeeded in her goal – but at the cost of
severe injuries and several weeks spent housebound.

This problem goes deeper than one might think. The standard
answer to it, from the proponents of goalsetting, is that these are
examples of people setting the *wrong* goals – overly ambitious or
overly narrow ones. Of course, it's true that some goals are wiser
than others. But the more profound hazard here affects virtually
any form of future planning. Formulating a vision of the future
requires, by definition, that you isolate some aspect or aspects of
your life, or your organisation, or your society, and focus on those
at the expense of others. But problems arise thanks to the law of

unintended consequences, sometimes expressed using the phrase 'you can never change only one thing'. In any even slightly complex system, it's extremely hard to predict how altering one variable will affect the others. 'When we try to pick out any thing by itself,' the naturalist and philosopher John Muir observed, 'we find it hitched to everything else in the universe.'

The thinker who probably pursued this notion further than anyone else was the anthropologist Gregory Bateson, who spent a significant part of his early career studying everyday life in the villages of Bali. These villages, he concluded, owed their social cohesion and effective functioning to customs and rituals that he described as 'non-maximizing'. He meant that these traditions had the effect of discouraging villagers from focusing on any one goal at the risk of a detrimental effect on others. A Balinese ethos of frugality, for example, was balanced with a custom of occasional ritual displays of conspicuous spending, thereby preventing the quest for wealth from damaging other social goals, and holding competitiveness and inequality among villagers in check. The obvious contrast was with Western industrialised societies, where maximising economic growth had become the goal to which all else was sacrificed. If life in America or Great Britain was best compared to climbing a ladder, life in rural Bali was more like an endless but graceful tightrope walk, resulting in a 'steady state' of social thriving geared to no particular set of goals. 'The continued existence of complex interactive systems', Bateson argued, 'depends upon preventing the maximization of any variable.' This need not be taken as an argument for abandoning all future planning whatsoever, but it serves as a warning not to strive too ardently for any single vision of the future. As Chris Kayes pointed out, the mountaineers who died climbing Everest in 1996 did success-fully reach their goal: they ascended to the summit. The tragic unintended consequence was that they didn't make it back down alive.

What might it mean to *turn towards* uncertainty – to learn to develop a tolerance for it, or even to embrace it? To try to answer this question, I first sought out a recovering goal addict who I'd heard had some radical ideas on the matter.

I met Steve Shapiro in a poorly lit bar in New York's West Village, where he was drinking a pint of Samuel Adams lager, working his way through a cheeseburger, and keeping half an eye on the baseball game on the corner television. There was nothing about his appearance, in other words, to suggest that he was anything but a quintessentially all-American forty-five-year-old. His job description might have given the same impression: he was a consultant who travelled the country running workshops with businesspeople. His life unfolded in conference suites, airport lounges, and hotel bars; PowerPoint was sometimes involved. Yet behind his quick smile and open features, the real Shapiro was a kind of enemy agent, because the message he delivered ran counter to some of the most deeply cherished ideologies of American corporate life. He argued in favour of giving up goals, and embracing uncertainty instead.

Shapiro did, in fact, start out as an all-American achiever, committed to his goal of becoming a highly paid management consultant. His punishing hours destroyed his marriage. 'I'm not sure if my goals drove me to work the crazy hours I did,' he later wondered, 'or if I used my goals as an excuse to avoid issues in my personal life.' He tried to dig himself out of such crises by means of even more goals (at one point, he recalled, he had a five-year plan to become 'a leader in the innovation space'). But none of these plans changed his life. What made the difference, in the end, was a conversation with a friend who told him he spent too much energy thinking about his future. He should think of himself more 'like a frog', she said. Shapiro was wondering whether to feel insulted when she explained: 'You should sun yourself on a lily-pad until you get bored; then, when the time is right, you should jump to a new lily-pad and hang out there for a while. Continue this over and over, moving in whatever direction feels right.' The imagery of sunbathing on lily-pads should not be taken to imply laziness. Shapiro's friend's point was entirely compatible with his hard-charging, achievement-hungry personality; it simply promised to channel it more healthily. In fact, it promised to help him achieve *more*, by permitting him to enjoy his work in the present, rather than postponing his happiness to a point five years in the future – whereupon, in any case, he would surely just replace his current five-year plan with another. The idea triggered a shift of perspective for Shapiro that would eventually lead to his reinvention as an advocate for abolishing goals.

Unsurprisingly, perhaps, the companies that pay Steve Shapiro for his advice have sometimes proved resistant to this idea. ('People looked at me pretty funny sometimes,' he said.) Chris Kayes has encountered similar opposition: 'At any company I visit,' he told me, 'there's always some manager who says, "You know, that stuff they did on Everest – taking huge risks, ignoring the consequences, ploughing on regardless – that's what I *want* people to be doing round here!"' Shapiro's counterargument to his sceptical clients begins with what he calls 'the happiness and self-worth side of things': goal-free living simply makes for happier humans. In survey research he commissioned, drawing on samples of American adults, 41 per cent of people agreed that achieving their goals had failed to make them any happier or had left them disillusioned, while 18 per cent said their goals had destroyed a friendship, a marriage, or another significant relationship. Moreover, 36 per cent said that the more goals they set for themselves, the more stressed they felt – even though 52 per cent said that one of their goals was to reduce the amount of stress in their lives.

Bosses are more frequently persuaded, though, by Shapiro's other argument: that getting rid of goals, or focusing on them less fixedly, is often also the best way to extract results from employees. He seduces them with anecdotes about the effectiveness of operating goallessly, such as the tale of the Formula One pit crew with which he worked, whose members were told that they would no longer be assessed on the basis of speed targets; they would be rated on style instead. Instructed to focus on acting 'smoothly', rather than on beating their current record time, they wound up performing faster. Then there was the story of the sales team that went from missing its targets to exceeding them – as soon as it became company policy to keep those targets a secret from the salespeople. 'You can have a broad sense of direction without a specific goal or a precise vision of the future,' Shapiro told me. 'I think of it like jazz, like improvisation. It's all about meandering with purpose.'

More recently, the benefits of a goal-free approach to business have started to be substantiated by more than mere anecdote. A few years ago, the researcher Saras Sarasvathy recruited forty-five entrepreneurs who met a predetermined definition of 'successful': they each had at least fifteen years' experience in starting businesses and had taken at least one company public. She presented them with a detailed hypothetical scenario about a potentially lucrative new software product. (Confusingly, it was software to help entrepreneurs launch businesses.) Sarasvathy then conducted two-hour-long interviews with each participant, probing how they might take this promising but vague idea and make real money from it. She generated hundreds of pages of interview transcripts – and then hundreds more when, for the purposes of comparison, she conducted a parallel exercise among executives at older, larger corporations.

We tend to imagine that the special skill of an entrepreneur lies in having a powerfully original idea and then fighting to turn that vision into reality. But the outlook of Sarasvathy's interviewees rarely bore this out. Their precise endpoint was often mysterious to them, and their means of proceeding reflected this. Overwhelmingly, they scoffed at the goals-first doctrine of Locke and Latham. Almost none of them suggested creating a detailed business plan or doing comprehensive market research to hone the details of the product they were aiming to release. ('I don't believe in market research,' one anonymous participant told Sarasvathy. 'Somebody once told me the only thing you need is a customer. Instead of asking all the questions, I'd try to make some sales.') The entrepreneurs didn't think like high-end chefs, concocting a vision of a dish and then hunting for the perfect ingredients. They behaved more like ordinary, time-pressed home cooks, checking what was in the fridge and the cupboards, then figuring out, on the fly, what they could make and how. 'I always live by the motto of "Ready, fire, aim",' said one. 'I think that if you spend too much time doing "Ready, aim, aim, aim", you're never going to see all the good things that would happen if you actually started doing it. I think business plans are interesting, but they have no real meaning, because you can't put in all the positive things that will occur.' The most valuable skill of a successful entrepreneur, Chris Kayes is convinced, isn't 'vision' or 'passion' or a steadfast insistence on destroying every barrier between yourself and some prize you're obsessed with. Rather, it's the ability to adopt an unconventional approach to learning: an improvisational flexibility not merely about which route to take towards some predetermined objective, but also a willingness to change the destination itself. This is a flexibility that might be squelched by rigid focus on any one goal.

Saras Sarasvathy has distilled her anti-goal approach into a set of principles she calls 'effectuation'. It is an outlook with implications far beyond the world of entrepreneurialism; it might serve as a worthy philosophy for life. 'Causally minded' people, to use Sarasvathy's terminology, are those who select or are given a specific goal, and then choose from whatever means are available to make a plan for achieving it. Effectually minded people, on the other hand, examine what means and materials are at their disposal, then imagine what possible ends or provisional next directions those means might make possible. The effectualists include the cook who scours the fridge for leftover ingredients; the chemist who figured out that the insufficiently sticky glue he had developed could be used to create the Post-it note; or the unhappy lawyer who realises that her spare-time photography hobby, for which she already possesses the skills and the equipment, could be turned into a job. One foundation of effectuation is the 'bird in hand' principle: 'Start with your means. Don't wait for the perfect opportunity. Start taking action, based on what you have readily available: what you are, what you know and who you know.' A second is the 'principle of affordable loss': Don't be guided by thoughts of how wonderful the rewards might be if you were spectacularly successful at any given next step. Instead – and there are distinct echoes, here, of the Stoic focus on the worst-case scenario – ask how big the loss would be if you failed. So long as it would be tolerable, that's all you need to know. Take that next step, and see what happens.

'See what happens', indeed, might be the motto of this entire approach to working and living, and it is a hard-headed message, not a woolly one. 'The quest for certainty blocks the search for meaning,' argued the social psychologist Erich Fromm. 'Uncertainty is the very condition to impel man to unfold his powers.' Uncertainty is where things happen. It is where the opportunities – for success, for happiness, for really living – are waiting.

'To be a good human,' concludes the American philosopher Martha Nussbaum, applying this perspective to her own field of ethics, 'is to have a kind of openness to the world, an ability to trust uncertain things beyond your own control, that can lead you to be shattered in very extreme circumstances for which you were not to blame. That says something very important about the ethical life: that it is based on a trust in the uncertainty, and on a willingness to be exposed. It's based on being more like a plant than a jewel: something rather fragile, but whose very particular beauty is inseparable from that fragility.'

5

Who's There?

How to Get Over Your Self

Why are you unhappy? Because 99.9 per cent of everything you think, and of everything you do, is for yourself – and there isn't one.

– Wei Wu Wei, *Ask the Awakened*

IF YOU HAD SPENT any time in the park that dominates Russell Square, in central London, in the late 1970s, it is possible that you might have noticed a skinny man aged around thirty, with delicate, almost elfin features, sitting alone on a park bench and doing absolutely nothing. For almost two years, if his own account is to be believed, Ulrich Tolle sat on park benches all day, unless it was raining or snowing hard; then he sought shelter in nearby public libraries. He spent his nights on the sofas of tolerant friends – or occasionally, when their tolerance expired, sleeping rough amid the bushes of Hampstead Heath. All things considered, though, it is unlikely that you'd have noticed him. Tolle was a nobody. And he would not have considered this label an insult, either, since from his perspective there was a sense in which it was literally true.

A few months prior to the beginning of his park-bench period, Tolle had been living alone in a bedsit in Belsize Park, in north-west London. He had recently completed a graduate degree at the University of London, and he was depressed to the point of regularly contemplating suicide. Then, the way he tells it, one night when he was filled with even more despair than usual, something snapped. Lying nearly paralysed on his bed in the dark, he underwent a terrifying, cataclysmic spiritual experience that, he claimed, erased his old identity completely. It was 'a slow movement at first', he wrote, many years later. 'I was gripped by an intense fear, and my body started to shake . . . I could feel myself being sucked into a void. It felt as if the void was inside myself, rather than outside. Suddenly, there was no more fear, and I let myself fall into that void. I have no recollection of what happened after that.' He lost consciousness.

When he awoke the next day, he knew instinctively that he was no longer the person he had been before. But what had happened seemed even more wrenching and elemental than that: somehow, in a way he couldn't properly put into words, it no longer felt as though he had a clearly bounded personal identity at all. His 'me' was missing in action. In its place, he felt only a sense of 'uninter-rupted deep peace and bliss', which faded a little after a while, but never went away. 'I walked around the city in utter amazement at the miracle of life on earth, as if I had just been born,' he wrote. After a while, he gave up the bedsit. With no personal agenda, no to-do list, no mental narrative telling him that he had to become someone or get anywhere other than what and who he was, he found that the idea of spending his days on the park benches of Russell Square didn't strike him as strange behaviour. There was no reason not to. And so, in a state of peaceful content-ment, he did.

Some time after his bedsit crisis, Ulrich Tolle changed his name to Eckhart Tolle, and began to speak and write about his experiences. Several years after that, another cataclysmic force – Oprah Winfrey – helped propel him to the position he enjoys today, as the world's bestselling living 'spiritual' author, with the arguable exception of the Dalai Lama. These facts do not enhance his credibility in everyone's eyes, and some sceptics have questioned his account of his transformation. Tolle says he doesn't mind the doubters, although you might argue that he doesn't have much choice: when you've told the world that you dwell in a realm of infinite equanimity, you can't start getting all snippy when people don't take you at your word.

You might also reasonably suspect that a figure such as Tolle would have little to contribute to the 'negative path' to happiness. The books that clutter the mind/body/spirit shelves, where his reside, often embody the very worst of the 'cult of optimism'. And Oprah's endorsement is no less troubling, given that it has also been bestowed upon the likes of *The Secret*, that epitome of magical positive thinking, as well as upon a number of questionable self-help gurus. Tolle's own first bestseller, *The Power of Now*, was once photographed under the arm of the socialite Paris Hilton as she prepared to serve a forty-five-day jail sentence in 2007. None of this bodes well. But regardless of exactly what happened to him that night in Belsize Park, his insights are worth considering because of his perspective on a topic that most of us, most of the time, take entirely for granted: the idea of the self.

In this book so far, we have explored the many ways in which conventional approaches to happiness and success seem to backfire, for the same essential reason: that there is something about trying to *make ourselves* happy and successful that is precisely what sabotages the attempt. But there is an even more unsettling possibility. What if the problem is not just one of technique?

What if we are mistaken not only about how to change ourselves but also about the nature of the selves we're trying to change? Calling into question our assumptions about what it means to talk about the self might prompt an entirely different approach to the psychology of happiness. And *The Power of Now* – which is, in fact, mercifully low on references to 'energy fields', 'vibrational frequencies', and the like – calls these assumptions into question with the title of its very first chapter: 'You Are Not Your Mind'. Think about that, if you dare.

The notion that our commonplace assumptions about selfhood might need re-examining certainly didn't originate with Eckhart Tolle. It is an ancient thought, central to Buddhism and to numerous other philosophical and religious traditions – a theme recurring so frequently in the history of religion and spirituality, in fact, that it is a part of what Aldous Huxley and others labelled 'the perennial philosophy'. Tolle was saying nothing new. But these reflections are often buried deep in ancient texts. I wanted to visit Tolle because he claimed to have experienced, at first hand, what this was all about. And he was willing to talk about it.

I had half assumed, perhaps even half hoped, that he might turn out to be a clichéd kind of guru, living in an ashram, fat and drunk on his own power, wearing elaborate robes and surrounded by adoring acolytes. It turned out, though, that he lived in a pleasant but slightly cramped top-floor apartment in a building in Vancouver, in Canada, just up the street from the campus of the University of British Columbia. He answered the door himself, stooping slightly. He was sixty now and birdlike, clad not in golden robes but in a strikingly unfashionable orange shirt and brown slacks. He indicated a leather armchair, on which I sat down, then seated himself on a sofa facing it, and waited for me to say something.

In Tolle's company, I soon learned, there was a lot of waiting. As on the benches of Russell Square, he seemed entirely comfortable with this, feeling no need to fill the silences, no pressure to move things along. I was less comfortable, because I couldn't think of anything sensible to say. Even 'How are you?', I had suddenly realised, was a potentially problematic opening question when the word 'you' – and what, exactly, that might mean – was the very thing I had come to discuss.

Few things seem so obvious, fundamental and undeniable as the self. Whatever uncertainties you might harbour about how to live – how to be happy, how to behave morally, what relationships to pursue, or what work to do – you probably retain the bedrock assumption that all these things are happening to an easily identifiable, single entity called you. This feels like such firm ground, in fact, that it forms the basis of what is arguably the most famous line in the history of Western philosophy: the seventeenth-century French philosopher René Descartes's dictum *Cogito ergo sum*: I think, therefore I am. There are very few aspects of our experience of being alive, Descartes realised, about which we can truly be certain. But we can be confident that we are us – that, in the most basic sense, we are who we take ourselves to be.

It is worth following Descartes's argument quite closely here. Imagine, he begins, an evil demon who is determined to play as many tricks on you as possible – a demon 'supremely powerful and cunning, [who] has devoted all his efforts to deceiving [you]'. How far could the demon's deceptions go? Don't forget, Descartes points out, that you rely for your entire understanding of the external world on your five senses: you can't know anything at all about what's going on outside your body unless you can touch, see, hear, smell, or taste it. And so, in principle, *everything* you think you know about that world might in fact be a breathtakingly detailed and convincing illusion, concocted by the evil demon. Looking out from inside your head, Descartes asks, how could you ever be completely certain that 'the sky, the air, the earth, colours, shapes, sounds and all external things' are not merely delusions, traps that the demon 'has laid for [your] credulity'? You might respond that such a scenario is absurdly unlikely, but Descartes is not concerned with its likelihood. He is employing the philosophical technique that came to be known as 'systematic doubt', attempting to isolate only that knowledge that he could regard as totally, unshakably certain.

Descartes's evil demon might go further still. (He is extremely evil, after all.) By sending the right sort of deceptive signals to your brain, he might even be responsible for your feeling that you possess a physical body. Maybe, in reality, you don't have a body. Maybe you're just a brain in a jar on a shelf in the demon's laboratory. How could you ever be sure? The parallels here with the 1999 movie *The Matrix* are not coincidental: that film is essentially a twentieth-century meditation on Descartes's seventeenth-century insights. 'A viewer of *The Matrix*', as the philosopher Christopher Grau puts it, 'is naturally led to wonder: how do I know I am not in the matrix? How do I know for sure the world is not a sophisticated charade, put forward by some superhuman intelligence in such a way that I cannot possibly detect the ruse?'

And yet despite all these possibilities for deception, there is exactly one thing and one thing only that cannot possibly be an illusion, Descartes maintains – and that is the fact that you are experiencing all this. Even the person who fears that he or she may be being fooled about literally everything else must know for sure that there is a 'him' or a 'her' who's being fooled. The demon couldn't fake that. 'The proposition "I think, therefore I am"', writes Descartes, 'is the first and most certain which presents itself to whoever conducts his thoughts in order.' You might not be able to know much with utter certainty. But you know that you are you. The sense of being you *can't* be an illusion – because 'you' is what's experiencing all these possibly illusory things in the first place. Somebody has to be there in order to be tricked.

Or do they? One of the first people to spot a potential flaw in this reasoning was a contemporary of Descartes, the French philosopher and priest Pierre Gassendi, who dedicated a significant part of his career to attempting – largely fruitlessly – to persuade Europe's intelligentsia that their star philosopher had got things badly wrong. Descartes's method of 'systematic doubt' had been intended to uproot every unwarranted assumption about the nature of experience. But hidden inside *Cogito ergo sum*, Gassendi argued, one final devilish assumption remained. Just because thinking is going on, that didn't mean Descartes was justified in concluding that thinking is being done by one particular unitary thinking agent – by an 'I'. As the German scientist Georg Lichtenberg would later phrase it, Descartes was entitled only to claim that 'thinking is occurring', not 'I think, therefore I am.'

It was the great Scottish philosopher David Hume, writing in the first half of the eighteenth century, who most vividly illustrated this hidden assumption, proposing a thought experiment of his own. Never mind systematic doubt, Hume suggested: instead, simply try turning your attention inwards, and trying to find this thing you call your self. Hume had made the attempt many times, he claimed, but he could never succeed. Instead of a self, all he ever found were specific processes: emotions, sensations, and thoughts. Where was the self that was feeling those emotions, sensing those sensations, and thinking those thoughts? Hume was stumped:

> For my part, when I enter most intimately into what I call myself, I always stumble on some particular perception or other, of heat or cold, light or shade, love or hatred, pain or pleasure. I can never catch myself at any time without a perception, and never can observe any thing but the perception. When my perceptions are remov'd for any time, as by sound sleep, so long I am insensible of myself, and may truly be said not to exist . . . If any one upon serious and unprejudic'd reflection, thinks he has a different notion of himself, I must confess I can reason no longer with him.

It isn't completely inconceivable, Hume concedes, that other people – possibly even all other people in the world, except him – do indeed have some kind of clearly identifiable, easily located self. The only interior world to which he has any direct access is David Hume's, so how could he ever hope to prove otherwise? But he doubts it. 'I may venture to affirm of the rest of mankind', he goes on, 'that they [too] are nothing but a bundle or collection of different perceptions, which succeed each other with an inconceivable rapidity, and are in perpetual flux and movement.'

Modern neuroscience has provided strong support for the suspicion that the self is not the 'thing' that we imagine it to be – that there is, in the words of the neuropsychologist Paul Broks, no 'centre in the brain where things do all come together'. One good illustration of this emerges from experiments involving patients with 'split brains' – people in whom the corpus callosum, which connects the left and right hemispheres of the brain, has been severed. As the psychologist Michael Gazzaniga has demonstrated, 'split-brain' people behave as if each of their hemispheres were its own independent self. In one study, the word 'walk' was projected only into the right side of a patient's brain. He got up and began to walk – but when asked why he had done so, the left side of his brain, responsible for language, quickly came up with a convincing reason: 'To get a Coke.' Each hemisphere seems capable of acting in those ways that we tend to associate with a 'self', casting doubt on the notion that there's any one region of the brain where such a thing might reside. The philosopher Julian Baggini points out that this isn't quite the same as saying that the self 'doesn't exist'; just because we may be a complex collection of things, instead of one simple thing, it doesn't follow that we are not real. A 'bundle of perceptions', to use Hume's phrase, is still a real bundle of perceptions. But the fact remains that we have been using a term and a concept – the self – that on closer inspection isn't at all what it seems.

Eckhart Tolle looked at me and blinked amiably.

'Thanks for sparing the time!' I began, a little hesitantly, before immediately berating myself for not remembering that 'time' was one of the things that Tolle claimed no longer to experience in a meaningful way. 'Time isn't precious at all,' he writes in *The Power of Now*, 'because it is an illusion.' Only the present, 'the now', is real.

More on this – ironically enough – later.

'It's really a pleasure,' he replied, blinking amiably again and waiting. This waiting and smiling and blinking was something I'd seen him do before, albeit at a distance. A few years previously,

Oprah Winfrey, while championing his books on her talk show, had enlisted him to take part in a ten-week online seminar video series, during which she repeatedly characterised him as a spiritual leader with the power to transform the consciousness of the planet. Tolle had just smiled and blinked. Winfrey seemed unnerved by his willingness to break one of the first rules of broadcasting: no long stretches of silence.

The voice in my head – the one that was, right at that moment, criticising me for still not having come up with a meaningful opening question – is something most of us notice only when we're stressed, as I definitely was. But the starting-point of Eckhart Tolle's philosophy – as he began to explain, once I'd finally phrased a question – is that we spend our whole lives in the company of such a voice. The voice judges and interprets reality, determines our emotional reactions, and chatters so constantly and so loudly that we come to identify with it: we imagine that we *are* the chattering stream of thinking. If you doubt this account of what it's like inside your mind, consider the possibility that this might be because you're too closely identified with the chatter to notice. 'There is this complete identification with the thoughts that go through your head,' Tolle said, his accent betraying a trace of his native Germany, when I asked him what he thought was the biggest barrier to happiness for most people. 'It's just a total absence of awareness, except for the thoughts that are continuously passing through your mind. It is the state of being so identified with the voices in your head' – and at this point he emitted a tight Germanic chuckle – 'that you think you *are* the voices in your head.'

In his book *A New Earth*, Tolle recounts an outwardly insignificant incident that occurred some months before his terrifying nocturnal experience in the Belsize Park bedsit. It was the first time he realised how closely identified he was with his thinking. At that time, he was studying in the central library of the University of London, and would travel there on the Underground each morning, shortly after rush hour:

One time, a woman in her early thirties sat opposite me. I had seen her before a few times on that train. One could not help but notice her. Although the train was full, the seats on either side of her were unoccupied, the reason being, no doubt, that she appeared to be quite insane. She looked extremely tense, and talked to herself incessantly in a loud and angry voice. She was so absorbed in her thoughts that she was totally unaware, it seemed, of other people, or her surroundings . . . Her monologue went something like this: 'And then she said to me . . . so I said to her you are a liar . . . how dare you accuse me of . . . when you are the one who has always taken advantage of me . . . I trusted you and you betrayed my trust . . .'

The woman got off the train at Tolle's stop. Out of curiosity, he decided to follow her, until gradually he began to realise that she was heading for the university library, just like him. For Tolle, this was troubling. He was an ambitious and driven young graduate student who had come to think of academic research as a pinnacle of human activity, and of universities like his as being home to an élite class of accomplished, or at least aspiring, intellectuals. He remembered wondering: 'How could an insane person like her be part of this?'

I was still thinking about her when I was in the men's room, prior to entering the library. As I was washing my hands, I thought: 'I hope I don't end up like her.' The man next to me looked briefly in my direction, and I suddenly was shocked when I realised that I hadn't just thought those words, but mumbled them aloud. 'Oh, my God, I'm already like her,' I thought.

I squirmed when I first read this, recalling my own Stoic exercise in talking out loud on the London Underground. Back then, my intention had been to learn that I could tolerate embarrassment and live with the thought that other people might think me insane. Tolle was making a more radical point: that only a very thin line separates such 'insane' people from the rest of us. The main difference is that, most of the time, we non-insane people manage to keep our constant mental chatter inaudible to others.

It is when we identify with this inner chatter, Tolle suggests – when we come to think of it *as* us – that thinking becomes compulsive. We do it all the time, ceaselessly, and the idea that we might ever enjoy a respite from thinking never occurs to us. We come to see our thinking and our continuing to exist as people as one and the same thing. 'Not to be able to stop thinking is a dreadful affliction,' Tolle writes. 'But we don't realise this, because almost everybody is suffering from it. So it's considered normal.' The sense of self that we construct from identifying with our thoughts is what Tolle calls the 'ego'. (Different thinkers use this term in very different ways.) And by definition, living in the service of the ego can never make us happy.

Why can the ego never bring happiness? Tolle's argument here echoes the Stoics, who concluded that our judgments about the world are the source of our distress. But he takes things further, suggesting that these judgments, along with all our other thoughts, are what we take ourselves to be. We're not only distressed by our thoughts; we imagine that we *are* those thoughts. The ego that results from this identification has a life of its own. It sustains itself through dissatisfaction – through the friction it creates against the present moment, by opposing itself to what's happening, and by constantly projecting into the future, so that happiness is always some other time, never now. The ego, Tolle likes to say, thrives on drama, because compulsive thinking can sink its teeth into drama. The ego also thrives on focusing on the future, since it's much easier to think compulsively about the future than about the present. (It's really quite tricky, when you try it, to think compulsively about right now.) If all this is correct, we have inadvertently sentenced ourselves to unhappiness. Compulsive thinking is what we take to be the core of our being – and yet compulsive thinking relies on our feeling dissatisfied.

The way out of this trap is not to stop thinking – thinking, Tolle agrees, is exceedingly useful – but to *disidentify* from thoughts: to stop taking your thoughts to be you, to realise, in the words of *The Power of Now*, that 'you are not your mind'. We should start using the mind as a tool, he argues, instead of letting the mind use us, which is the normal state of affairs. When Descartes said 'I think, therefore I am,' he had not discovered 'the most fundamental truth', Tolle insists; instead, he had given expression to 'the most basic error'.

What Tolle claimed had happened to him with such force that night in his bedsit was precisely a disidentification from thinking. At the time, he had just graduated with a first-class master's degree in languages and history, and was preparing for a doctorate. 'I'd done well because I was motivated by fear of not being good enough,' he remembered. 'So I worked very hard.' He saw himself as an intellectual in the making, and was 'convinced that all the answers to the dilemmas of human existence could be found through the intellect – that is, by thinking'. But his intellectual labours weren't making him happy – and this realisation made him feel even worse. 'I lived in a state of almost continuous anxiety,' he wrote. Gradually, and then not so gradually, the anxiety was ratcheting up and up. Something had to give. And on that night, shortly after his twenty-ninth birthday, it did:

> I woke up in the early hours with a feeling of absolute dread. I had woken up with such a feeling many times before, but this time it was more intense than it had ever been. The silence of the night, the vague outlines of the furniture in the dark room, the distant noise of a passing train – everything felt so alien, so hostile, and so utterly meaningless that it created in me a deep loathing of the world. The most loathsome thing of all, however, was my own existence . . . I could feel that a deep longing for annihilation, for non-existence, was now becoming much stronger than the instinctive desire to continue to live. 'I cannot live with myself much longer.' This was the thought that kept repeating itself in my mind.

'I cannot live with myself': the phrase is a cliché, but Tolle was stopped dead by its implications. 'If I cannot live with myself,' he remembered thinking, 'there must be two of me: the "I" and the "self" that "I" cannot live with. Maybe, I thought, only one of them is real. I was so stunned by this realisation that my mind stopped. I was conscious, but there were no more thoughts.' And then, before he knew it, it was morning – the morning that he felt suffused with a feeling of 'uninterrupted deep peace and bliss'. What had happened, if his account is to be believed, was that he no longer mistakenly believed he *was* his thinking; he saw himself, instead, as the witness to it. This is an experience you can easily taste for yourself by deliberately deciding to watch your own thinking. Sit like a cat at a mouse-hole, Tolle advises, waiting to see what your next thought will be. 'When you listen to a thought,' he explains, 'you are aware not only of the thought, but also of yourself as the witness of the thought. A new dimension of consciousness has come in. As you listen to the thought, you feel a conscious presence – your deeper self – behind or underneath the thought, as it were. The thought then loses its power over you, and quickly subsides, because you are no longer energising the mind through identification with it. This is the beginning of the end of involuntary and compulsive thinking.' We have all experienced something 'behind or underneath' thought, in those moments that thinking seems temporarily to fall away: when gasping in awe at beautiful scenery, after intense physical exercise, or while making love. The trick is to take that stance towards thinking all the time, even when you're thinking. If any this sounds familiar, it may be because it leads back to Buddhism. Watching your thoughts in this way is a form of meditation.

This is the point at which Tolle's outlook gets especially tricky for a sceptic to swallow. He seems to assume that when you stop identifying with your ego, you discover who you *really* are – that you discover your 'deeper self' or your 'true Being', which was hiding behind the fake self all along. But this kind of talk rightly makes more mainstream philosophers nervous. Just because you have succeeded in dismantling the conventional understanding of the self, it doesn't necessarily follow that you'll find the 'real' one. Perhaps we are just a 'bundle of perceptions', as Hume put it. Perhaps there is no 'deeper', 'truer' meaning to the notion of who we are. Once again, though, this isn't a question that we need to answer conclusively. Merely asking it is what matters. It is enough, for now, to enquire within: don't you feel a certain tranquility when you seek to become the witness to your thoughts, rather than identifying with them completely?

The optimism-focused, goal-fixated, positive-thinking approach to happiness is exactly the kind of thing the ego loves. Positive thinking is all about identifying with your thoughts, rather than disidentifying from them. And the 'cult of optimism' is all about looking forward to a happy or successful future, thereby reinforcing the message that happiness belongs to some other time than now. Schemes and plans for making things better fuel our dissatisfaction with the only place where happiness can ever be found – the present. 'The important thing,' Tolle told me, 'is not to be continuously lost in this mental projection away from now. Most humans are never fully present in the now, because unconsciously they believe that the next moment must be more important than this one. But then you miss your whole life, which is never not now.' Another staccato chuckle. 'And that's a revelation for some people. To realise that your whole life is only ever now. Many people suddenly realise that they have lived most of their life as if this were not true – as if the opposite were true.' Without noticing we're doing it, we treat the future as intrinsically more valuable than the present. And yet the future never seems to arrive.

Instead of seeking ways to solve your problems in the future, it can be illuminating to try asking yourself if you have any problems right now. The answer, unless you're currently in physical pain, is very likely to be no. Most problems, by definition, involve thoughts about how something might turn out badly in the future, whether in five minutes or in five years, or thoughts about things that happened in the past. It can be curiously difficult to identify any problems that afflict you at this very moment, in the present – and it is always the present.

Or consider the fraught topic of self-esteem. We tend to assume that having high self-esteem is a good thing, but some psychologists have long suspected that there might be something wrong with the whole notion – because it rests on the assumption of a unitary, easily identifiable self. Setting out to give your 'self' one universal positive rating may in fact be deeply perilous. The problem lies in the fact that you're getting into the self-rating game at all; implicitly, you're assuming that you are a single self that can be given a universal grade. When you rate your self highly, you actually *create* the possibility of rating your self poorly; you are reinforcing the notion that your self is something that can be 'good' or 'bad' in the first place. And this will always be a preposterous overgeneralisation. You have strengths and weaknesses; you behave in good ways and bad ways. Smothering all these nuances with a blanket notion of self-esteem is a recipe for misery. Inculcate high self-esteem in your children, claims Paul Hauck, a psychologist opposed to the concept of self-esteem, and you will be 'teaching them arrogance, conceit and superiority' – or alternatively, when their high self-esteem falters, 'guilt, depression, [and] feelings of inferiority and insecurity' instead. Better to drop the generalisations. Rate your individual acts as good or bad, if you like. Seek to perform as many good ones, and as few bad ones, as possible. But leave your self out of it.

One final implication of thinking about selfhood in this way – and arguably the most significant one – concerns the idea of selflessness. We know from personal experience, and now from decades of psychology studies, that helping other people is a far more reliable strategy for happiness than focusing solely on yourself. One of the more distasteful aspects of positive thinking – and of conventional approaches to happiness in general – is the way in which they seem to encourage self-absorption. Then again, 'selfless' approaches to happiness can lead us into a conceptual muddle: if you take on a weekly volunteering assignment, say, with the aim of becoming happier, are you being selfless at all? Do you have to make yourself *miserable* in order to be truly self-less? The questions go on and on. Perhaps the answer to all these conundrums isn't to act selfishly or selflessly, but to question the notion of the self on which those distinctions are based. Both 'selfish' and 'selfless' activities are liable to end up merely feeding the ego, which thrives on dissatisfaction. Loosen your grip on selfhood itself, Tolle argues, and you'll stand a far better chance of cultivating happiness – your own and other people's – without the distraction of ego.

It's quite possible that all this simply leaves you cold – that it fails to chime in any way with your own inner experience. If that's the case, there is one more angle from which it can be demonstrated that selfhood is not all that it seems. This argument takes the form of an extended thought experiment, which I've adapted here from the work of the self-styled 'spiritual entertainer' Alan Watts. A bearded, plummy-voiced Englishman who made his home on the West Coast of the United States, and who died in 1973, Watts didn't have any breakthrough insights of his own. He was a populariser, intent on explaining the philosophies of the East to the populations of the West. Few professional philosophers today would consider him worthy of their title. But his insights – which rely on no New Agery nor pseudoscience at all, just rigorous, rational thinking – may, in a surprisingly enjoyable way, warp your mind.

Watts begins with what seems like an utterly straightforward question: What do you take to be the boundary of yourself – the place where you end and where 'the rest of the world' that isn't you begins? For most of us, the answer, as he puts it, is that we think of ourselves as 'packages of skin'. It is the envelope of skin enclosing the physical body that defines the boundary of our selves.

You might spot one immediate problem with this. Sometimes, when we use the word 'me', we seem to be using a different definition – one in which 'me' refers not to the whole body, but only to something inside the head. According to this definition, the rest of the body isn't 'me' to the same degree as the head. Suppose your foot had to be amputated: would you consider that you had become less 'yourself'? (Probably not – but if your *head* had to be amputated, things would be remarkably different.) Already, then, we seem to have two rival definitions of precisely what physical matter we're referring to when we refer to 'me'. But let's stick with the 'packages of skin' definition for now.

Suppose you were to zoom in, using an ultra-powerful microscope, on a part of your left hand, until all that you were looking at was a tiny region of your index finger, and a tiny part of the air surrounding it. Given sufficient magnification, what you would see through the microscope would be nothing but a cacophony of molecules: some making up your finger and some making up the adjacent air. Which brings us to the next question – or really the same question, in rephrased form. What exactly is your rationale for drawing a boundary between some of these molecules and others, so as to define some of them as 'you', and some of them as the world outside you? At this magnification, it's readily apparent that all we're talking about is molecules, after all. What makes some of them so special as to count as 'you'?

One obvious answer that springs to mind has to do with conscious control. You seem to be able to choose to move your index finger, for example, in a way that simply doesn't apply to things outside your skin. Perhaps this, then, is why the skin boundary is so important: on one side of it, you have conscious control; on the other side of it, you don't. But Watts has a ready response to that. Do you really exert conscious control, he wonders, over your breathing? Do you actively and consciously pump the blood through your veins, or dispatch antibodies to fight viral infections? You don't: those things just happen. Even thinking itself – as I had come to understand so acutely at the Insight Meditation Society – isn't as voluntary as we might like to imagine. Most of the time, thinking just seems to happen.

Fair enough, you might reply; perhaps I shouldn't have said *conscious* control. Unconscious control is plainly part of it, too. Whether consciously or unconsciously, I control everything inside my skin, and nothing outside it. Except, of course, that's not true, either: you exert control over plenty of things that are outside your skin. Using the right tools, you can build a swimming pool in your back garden; using your powers of persuasion, you might persuade hundreds of thousands of people to depose a dictator. You might argue that this is different – that it's an *indirect* form of control, while the control that you exert over your limbs feels more direct. But Watts wouldn't let you get away with that objection, because it relies on circular reasoning: it presumes an answer to the very conundrum that we're engaged in trying to untangle. After all, the distinction between 'direct' control and 'indirect' control is defined by nothing more or less than where you draw the boundary between 'yourself' and the rest of the world. And it is exactly this boundary – and whether we truly have good reason for drawing it where we traditionally draw it – that is at issue.

By now, the awkwardness of your situation ought to be apparent. Whatever criterion you propose as the basis for drawing the boundary between 'you' and 'not you', there seems to be a counterargument which, at the very least, throws the matter into doubt. It is at this point that Watts reveals the most disorienting part of his argument. Encountering it for the first time – I speak from experience – can be a little like ambling to the top of a gentle hill only to discover that its brow is also the precipice of a sheer, high cliff, dropping down to crashing waves below.

The argument goes as follows: that no matter where you draw the boundary – even if we could agree on a place at which to draw it – you would not really be drawing a boundary in the conventional sense at all. Because (here it comes) the very notion of a boundary line depends on it having two sides. When you think about it, it doesn't make much sense to describe a boundary as something that keeps two things apart. It makes more sense to describe it as the place at which they meet – or, more accurately, the place at which *they are exactly the same thing*. The inside of the boundary relies for its very existence on the outside, and vice versa; they are, inextricably and by definition, part of the same whole. You simply can't have the peak of a wave without the trough, or darkness without light.

This is the insight behind the ancient Chinese symbol of yin and yang, but there is nothing religious or even especially 'spiritual' about it. It is merely the conclusion, Watts argues, to which rigorous thinking must lead. There cannot be a 'you' without an 'everything else', and attempting to think about one in isolation from the other makes no sense. Nor is this some vague, insipid, flowers-and-incense observation about how 'we are all one'. It holds true on every level, from the most abstract to the most concrete. Yes, it is true that you wouldn't be you without the relationships you're in or the community to which you belong. But you also wouldn't be you if it weren't for all the physical objects in the world that aren't you.

We spend our lives failing to realise this obvious truth, and thus anxiously seeking to fortify our boundaries, to build our egos and assert our superiority over others, as if we could separate ourselves from them, without realising that interdependence makes us what we are. 'Really,' Watts wrote, 'the fundamental, ultimate mystery – the only thing you need to know to understand the deepest metaphysical secrets – is this: that for every outside, there is an inside, and that for every inside, there is an outside, and although they are different, they go together.'

That phrase 'they are different' is important. The case being made here is not that boundaries don't exist – that the 'true' way to perceive the world would be as some big, boundary-less mess of stuff, like half-melted ice cream. The fact that 'you' and 'everything else' are intrinsically interconnected needn't mean you don't exist. Our sanity depends on maintaining a coherent sense of self, and on setting healthy boundaries between ourselves and others – and neither Alan Watts nor Eckhart Tolle wishes to imperil your sanity. Instead, the conclusion to which both their thinking leads is that the self is best thought of as some kind of a fiction, albeit an extremely useful one – and that realising this, instead of doing everything we can to deny it, might be the route to fulfilment.

Others have remarked on the way that Eckhart Tolle's quiet presence seems to burn up people's scepticism, and this applied to me, too. Reluctant though I was to admit it, he really did seem to exude a palpable stillness, which seeped into the corners of the small Vancouver apartment and eventually, by the end of an afternoon's conversation, into me. The silences that had felt so awkward when I arrived slowly became more tolerable, then actually enjoyable, as my compulsion to fill them with talking began to subside. For long stretches of seconds, Tolle blinked and smiled, and I found myself smiling comfortably back.

Yet, still, I couldn't quite bring myself to believe that his inner life was as marvellously tranquil as he claimed. When, I wondered, was the last time that he had become really irritated? 'I can't remember the last time it happened,' he replied. 'I think maybe it was . . . ' Earlier today? Yesterday? 'I think it was a few months ago,' he said, after a while. 'I remember that I was walking outside, and there was this big dog, and the owner wasn't controlling it – it was pestering a smaller dog. And I felt a wave of irritation. But [the irritation] doesn't stick around, because it is not perpetuated by thought activity. It only lasted moments.' In *The Power of Now*, Tolle writes admiringly of watching ducks in a pond near his home, and what happens when they get into a fight. They tussle, but then, the confrontation over, they flap their wings and ruffle their feathers, as if to shake off the memory of the encounter. Then they swim peacefully once more. Ducks bear no grudges. People, with egos, do. Indeed, when Tolle hits his stride, there is no human outrage afflicting the world that he is not willing to attribute to our efforts to defend and strengthen our egos. War, tyrannies, and injustices of all kinds stand exposed as little but the efforts of insecure egos to fortify themselves: to harden their boundaries, to separate themselves, and to impose upon the rest of the world the thought patterns on which they have come to imagine that their very lives – although, in reality, only their egos – depend.

When I finally rose to leave the apartment, I hesitated for a moment – for some reason, shaking Tolle's hand seemed inappropriately formal – when he suddenly stepped forward and enveloped me in a bear hug. Then I took the lift to the ground floor, called a taxi, and sat on the wrought-iron bench outside the building, waiting to be collected. I felt curiously light-headed and peaceful, and it occurred to me that it might not be such a bad thing to stay sitting on that bench, in the fading light, doing nothing in particular, for several more hours. But that wasn't an option. I – whatever *that* meant – had to get to the airport in time for my plane home.

6

The Safety Catch

The Hidden Benefits of Insecurity

Security is a kind of death, I think.
– Tennessee Williams, 'The Catastrophe of Success'

ON 13 JANUARY 2002, during the edgy, watchful months following the terrorist attacks of 9/11, a pilot named Elwood Menear – 'Woodie', to his friends – arrived at Philadelphia's International Airport. The forty-six-year-old was due to fly a routine domestic journey to Minneapolis on behalf of his employer, US Airways, and he had no grounds for imagining that his name might soon be making the headlines alongside that weekend's other most memorable news story, which involved President Bush choking on a pretzel.

Security screening procedures at Philadelphia, in common with those across America and the rest of the world, were becoming progressively tighter. Less than a month previously, Richard Reid, the would-be 'shoe bomber', had been tackled and subdued on board a flight from Paris to Miami, thereby initiating the era of compulsory shoe-checking for all travellers. Pilots were not excused all these rigorous new checks, and when Woodie Menear's turn came, the security screener expressed concern about the presence of a pair of tweezers in his cabin baggage. As it happened, tweezers – unlike corkscrews or metal scissors, for example – were not on the list of forbidden items; Menear was not breaching regulations by trying to bring them on board. But the official paused just long enough to spark frustration on the part of the pilot, who, like his colleagues, had been growing ever more exasperated by each new restriction. This time it was too much. Menear did not explode in rage; he merely asked a sarcastic question. But it was one that would lead to his immediate arrest, a night in jail, his suspension by US Airways, and months of legal wranglings before he was finally acquitted of 'making terroristic threats' and permitted to return to his job.

'Why are you worried about tweezers,' Menear asked, 'when I could crash the plane?'

Given the time and the place, it was an idiotic thing to say. But the insight that it crystallised was anything but idiotic. As aviation security restrictions grew more and more intricate in the years after Menear's arrest – culminating in the 2006 European ban on all but the tiniest of quantities of liquids in carry-on luggage – critics grew more strident in pointing out that the logic behind the whole policy seemed flawed. It made sense, of course, to keep guns and other weapons out of aeroplane cabins. But those had been prohibited for years. Beyond that, the new rules seemed destined to cause great inconvenience for millions of innocent passengers while doing very little to eliminate the risks posed by a dedicated hijacker. What 9/11 had shown, these critics argued, was not that light-duty 'boxcutter' utility knives were the next frontier in terrorism. What it had shown was that a terrorist who had reconciled himself to suicide would always have the upper hand against people who were unwilling to die – no matter which specific objects had been banned.

Bruce Schneier, an American security consultant who is one of the fiercest opponents of the post-9/11 crackdown, has made a name – and a few enemies – for himself by explaining the many ways in which one could easily hijack or bomb an aeroplane today, in spite of all the new measures. Garottes, for example, can be improvised from fishing line or dental floss, while the snapped-off handle of a wheeled bag makes 'a pretty effective spear'. Alternatively, you could buy some steel epoxy glue from a hard-ware store: it comes in two tubes, one containing steel dust and the other containing hardener, which you could combine in-flight, and mould into a stubby steel knife, using a metal teaspoon as a handle. (Neither steel epoxy glue nor metal teaspoons are prohibited on planes – unlike, say, snow globes, which are banned under American regulations.) Schneier's point is not, of course, that wheeled bags and dental floss should be urgently added to the list of items forbidden in flight. It is that you cannot make air travel significantly safer by banning each new item that a terrorist thinks to use, or that you fear he might, unless you're willing to ban *every* item – and perhaps also to force passengers to be strapped into their seats, too, given that hijackers could always use their bare hands. Not long after the 9/11 attacks, a reporter asked Schneier whether any measures could be taken that might guarantee that such a tragedy would never happen again. Sure, Schneier replied: just ground all the planes.

'There are precisely two things that have made air travel safer since 9/11: locks on cockpit doors, and teaching passengers that they have to fight back,' Schneier told me. He is forty-nine and ponytailed, and speaks in the quiet tones of someone who is confident of the truth of his opinions, and not especially concerned about winning you over. 'You can argue that there's a third – sky marshals. But actually, once you tell people you have them, you don't really need them. It's the *idea* of sky marshals that makes us safer, not the marshals themselves.'

If what Schneier says is correct, then an obvious question follows: Why do governments continue to impose these expensive and time-consuming restrictions? Why carry on playing a cat-and-mouse game with terrorists, in which the terrorists will always be one step ahead? There are many possible answers to this question, having to do with the pressure that politicians and safety officials feel to show that they are doing something, and to impress those who elect them or pay their salaries. But at the root of it all, Schneier argues, is the fundamental human desire for a *feeling* of safety and security – even though this feeling may be only indirectly related, at best, to *being* more safe or secure. Schneier coined the term 'security theatre' to refer to all those measures that are designed primarily to increase the feeling of security, without actually making people more secure. Indeed, it is perfectly possible to argue – Schneier has often done so – that security theatre in fact makes us *less* secure. It swallows resources that might otherwise be expended on more effective anti-terrorism measures, such as intelligence-gathering, and it makes passengers and security staff less alert to the kinds of suspicious behaviour they ought to be noticing. After all, if everyone's luggage is being so scrupulously examined that even snow globes are being intercepted, it might be easy to assume that you could let your guard down.

Start to look at security through Bruce Schneier's eyes, and some of the ways in which society approaches the issue begin to appear profoundly ridiculous. In 2007, for example, Britain's then prime minister, Gordon Brown, announced a barrage of measures to beef up security at the nation's airports, railway stations, and other transport hubs, including the construction of blast-resistant barriers. A posting on Schneier's blog explained that the barriers would be constructed at Liverpool Lime Street, that city's primary rail station, but that they would not be constructed at less busy suburban commuter stations, a few miles along the same stretch of track. The blog post was headlined: 'UK Spends Billions to Force Rail Terrorists to Drive a Little Further'. Brown's announcement was a classic piece of security theatre: a costly way to make travellers *feel* safer – so long as they didn't reflect too closely on the details – while doing nothing to deter an even slightly diligent terrorist.

In this book so far, we have seen how some of the most basic doctrines that dominate our thinking about happiness fail to work because we struggle for them too strenuously. It's easy to see how Bruce Schneier's critique of air security bears a superficial resemblance to this argument: in reality, many of the things we believe make air travel more secure don't do so, or make things worse. But the connection goes deeper – because 'security' in the context of air travel is really only one facet of a much bigger question that brings us to the heart of the 'negative' approach to happiness. The desire for a feeling of security and safety doesn't only lead us into irrationality in the field of counterterrorism. It leads us into irrationality all the time.

As we'll see, a staggering proportion of human activity – in politics, business, and international relations, as much as in our personal lives – is motivated by the desire to feel safe and secure. And yet this quest to feel secure doesn't always lead to security, still less to happiness. It turns out to be an awkward truth about psychology that people who find themselves in what the rest of us might consider conditions of extreme insecurity – such as

severe poverty – discover insights into happiness from which the
rest of us could stand to learn. And if the most radical proponents
of the 'negative path' are to be believed, in turning towards insecurity we may come to understand that security itself is a kind
of illusion – and that we were mistaken, all along, about what it
was we thought we were searching for.

It is easy to feel, these days, that we live in uniquely insecure
times, and that things are only going to get worse. Several years
ago, the 2020 Project, an initiative of the American intelligence
services charged with making broad forecasts about the future,
published a report with a chapter bluntly entitled 'Pervasive
Insecurity'. By 2020, the project's analysts wrote, 'we foresee a
more pervasive sense of insecurity, which may be as much based
on psychological perception as physical threats.' Among the chief
causes for anxiety, they predicted, would be 'concerns over job
security', 'fears revolving around migration', 'terrorism and
internal conflicts', and even 'conflicts among great powers'. And
all of that was written some time before the financial collapse of
the late 2000s, which brought a new wave of insecurity to millions.

Yet it is easy, too, to find evidence that people have *always*
believed that they are living in times of unique insecurity. In 1951
– a relatively happy and prosperous moment, all things considered,
after the deepest pain of the post-war recovery and before the worst
of the Cold War – Alan Watts captured his era's sense of insecurity
well. There was, he wrote, 'the feeling that we live in a time of
unusual insecurity. In the past hundred years or so, many long-
established traditions have broken down – traditions of family,
and social life, of government, of the economic order, and of
religious belief. As the years go by, there seem to be fewer and fewer
rocks to which we can hold, fewer things which we can regard as
absolutely right and true, and fixed for all time.' Then again, that

was how plenty of people felt in 634 BC in Rome, as well, when they were convinced that the city was destined to collapse after 120 years of existence. It is how people have felt at countless points in history since then. Try searching Google's library of digitised manuscripts for the phrase 'these uncertain times', and you'll find that it occurs over and over, in hundreds of journals and books, in virtually every decade the database encompasses, reaching back to the seventeenth century. 'As a matter of fact,' Watts insisted, 'our age is no more insecure than any other. Poverty, disease, war, change and death are nothing new.'

So people have always wanted to feel more secure than they do. Yet as Bruce Schneier's work in the field of air security helps to demonstrate, there's an enormous pitfall waiting for us – because the strategies that are designed to bestow a *feeling* of security often don't actually leave us more secure. They may even have the opposite effect. 'Security is both a feeling and a reality,' as Schneier puts it, 'and they're not the same.'

The feeling and the reality of security diverge in specific and predictable ways. Much has been written in recent years about 'cognitive biases' – the ways in which our judgments about reality tend to depart from reality itself – and many of these help explain the chronic mistakes we make when it comes to security. For example, we habitually fear threats from other humans more than threats from the natural world. We fear threats that we can easily call vividly to mind more than those we find difficult to picture – the so-called availability bias. We fear situations in which we feel as though we have no control, such as flying as a passenger on an aeroplane, more than situations in which we feel as if we have control, such as when at the steering wheel of a car. No wonder, then, that we sometimes risk making ourselves less secure by chasing feelings of security. You're vastly more likely to be killed as the result of a car crash than an air crash, and vastly more likely to die of heart disease than at the hands of a violent intruder. But if you react to news stories about air terrorism by taking the car when you'd otherwise have taken a plane, or if you spend time and energy protecting your home from attackers that you could have spent on improving your diet, you'll be letting your biases guide you towards a greater *feeling* of security at the expense of your real safety.

Psychologists are not unanimous about why these biases should have developed in the first place, but Schneier makes the plausible argument that the explanation lies in evolution – specifically, the discrepancy between the rate of evolutionary change and the rate at which modern society has developed. Adopting the long view of our species, across evolutionary time, it is easy to see that these biases might once have served our survival well – but that they fail us now because we confront situations for which they were never intended. Some animals, surprised by a car's headlights, may leap wildly from one side of the road to the other, in an instinctive effort to throw off the predator, which doesn't work when your predator is a 4 × 4. And 'like a squirrel whose predator-evasion techniques fail when confronted by a car,' observes Schneier, 'or a passenger pigeon who finds that evolution prepared him to survive the hawk but not the shotgun, our innate capabilities to deal with risk fail when confronted with things such as modern human society, technology, and the media.'

Take, for example, the availability bias. Caring more about those threats that you can picture vividly might, long ago, have made sense: the reason you could picture them vividly, most likely, was because they occurred a few yards away, in the village where you lived, and very recently. They really did pose a more serious risk, so the bias was a useful shortcut for making an accurate threat assessment. But if the reason that they are mentally 'available' to you today is that you're in the habit of watching a daily news bulletin, the very purpose of which is to scour the globe for the most lurid scenes of mayhem, you will be misled into focusing your worry on threats you don't actually face. Seeing a television report of a terrorist attack on foreign soil, you might abandon plans for an overseas holiday, in order to hang on to your feeling of safety – when, in truth, spending too much time sitting on the sofa watching television might pose a far greater threat to your survival.

If cognitive biases were the only problem with the quest for safety and security, the solution might be straightforward, if not necessarily easy to implement: it would simply be a matter of bearing the biases in mind and doing our best to adjust our behaviours accordingly. We would then avoid being misled by our evolved emotional responses; we'd achieve the protection from danger that we had been seeking, and perfect happiness would follow. Needless to say, it isn't that simple. The more radical possibility – the one that takes us to the core of the 'negative' approach to happiness – is that there might be something more fundamentally problematic about the goal of security; and that real happiness might be dependent on being willing to face, and to tolerate, insecurity and vulnerability.

This is a thorny topic. You'd have to be insane to argue that it was preferable to live in conditions of serious danger, or that a certain basic sense of psychological security isn't a healthy thing to possess. (The terminology creates additional confusion, since you could argue that anyone who is able calmly to tolerate feelings of insecurity and vulnerability must already be, by definition, rather secure to begin with.) But a recurring theme in the study

of happiness is that many of the ways in which we try to feel
'safe' don't ultimately make us happy. We seek financial security,
yet above a certain threshold level, more money doesn't translate
into more happiness. We protect ourselves from physical danger
by moving to safer neighbourhoods, or even locking ourselves
inside gated communities, but the effects of such trends on
community life have been demonstrated to have a negative effect
on collective levels of happiness. We seek the fulfilment of strong
romantic relationships and friendships, yet striving too hard to
achieve security in such relationships stifles them; their flourishing
depends on a certain degree of *not* being protected, of being open
to experiences both negative and positive. It is possible to be
similarly protected from terrorism, as Schneier said, so long as
you are happy to shut down the possibility of air travel itself.
What all these examples have in common is that achieving perfect
security would run counter to our interests. We might think we
want security more than anything, but when it comes down to
it, we don't.

'To be vulnerable', argue the psychotherapists Hal and Sidra
Stone, 'is to be without defensive armour, to be authentic and
present . . . when we are able to feel our vulnerability, we are able
to experience the full range of our reactions to the world around
us.' The point, says Brené Brown, a professor of social work who
has studied the psychological benefits of vulnerability, is that 'you
can't selectively numb emotion. You can't say: here's the bad stuff;
here's vulnerability, here's grief, here's shame, here's fear, here's
disappointment: I don't want these.' In the end, the only way you
can achieve protection from the negatives is by achieving protection from the positives, too – whereupon you realise that you
didn't really want such protection at all. Or as C. S. Lewis put it,
more poetically:

To love at all is to be vulnerable. Love anything and your heart will be wrung, and possibly broken. If you want to make sure of keeping it intact, you must give your heart to no-one, not even an animal. Wrap it carefully round with your hobbies and little luxuries; avoid all entanglements; lock it up safe in the casket or coffin of your selfishness. But in that casket – safe, dark, motionless, airless – it will change. It will not be broken; it will become unbreakable, impenetrable, irredeemable.

Becoming numb to negative emotions, Brown's research illustrates, doesn't even work as a way of protecting yourself from negative emotions themselves – for reasons that the Catholic monk and writer Thomas Merton expressed in his autobiography *The Seven Storey Mountain*. 'The truth that many people never understand', he wrote, 'is that the more you try to avoid suffering, the more you suffer, because smaller and more insignificant things begin to torture you, in proportion to your fear of being hurt.' Seen this way, it becomes clear that security-chasing is a large part of the problem with the 'cult of optimism'. Through positive thinking and related approaches, we seek the safety and solid ground of certainty, of knowing how the future will turn out, of a time in the future when we'll be ceaselessly happy and never have to fear negative emotions again. But in chasing all that, we close down the very faculties that permit the happiness we crave.

For the American Buddhist nun Pema Chödrön, insecurity is the essential nature of reality – and all our distress arises from trying to scramble to solid ground that doesn't actually exist. 'Becoming a Buddhist', she says, 'is about becoming homeless.' To turn to face reality is to see that we exist in a condition of 'fundamental groundlessness'. Yet most of us chronically 'scramble not to feel that groundlessness . . . my whole training [is] that there is no way to tie up those loose ends'. She goes on: 'You're never going to erase the groundlessness. You're never going to have a neat, sweet little picture with no messiness.' Chödrön's most famous book is entitled *When Things Fall Apart*, which makes it sound as though it might be a manual for getting back on a secure footing when things go catastrophically wrong. In fact, her point is that when things fall apart, however painful the experience, it's a good thing; the collapse of your apparent security represents a confrontation with life as it really is. 'Things are not permanent, they don't last, there is no final security,' she says. What makes us miserable is not this truth, but our efforts to escape it.

At this point, though, a weighty objection to all this might be troubling you in the same way that it troubled me. It's all very well for those of us who find ourselves in relatively comfortable situations to praise insecurity and vulnerability. We may be fortunate enough to live out our entire lives without encountering insecurity in its most acute forms. But what do you learn about happiness when insecurity really is the unavoidable background condition of your daily life?

It was a Sunday morning in January, cloudless and hot, and many of the residents of Africa's second-largest urban slum were dressed for church: the men in well-pressed suits, the women in dresses of fuchsia and bright green, children clutching Bibles. Here in the poorest part of Kibera – across the rubbish-strewn railway tracks that divided the slum proper from the rest of the Kenyan capital of Nairobi – it was a challenge to keep your church clothes clean as you picked your way along the muddy paths that passed for roads; in many places, the ground was composed of discarded plastic bags and other detritus. Between homes made from scraps of sheet metal and mud, chickens and dogs wandered through gullies that flowed with raw sewage.

Most of the churchgoers were heading up the hill to the big Africa Inland church, or across to the main Catholic one. There were numerous other tiny shop-front churches, too, hidden among the homes – dark one-room shacks in which a minister could be seen preaching to an audience of two or three, or playing hymns on a Casio keyboard. But in the opinion of Frankie Oluoch, a twenty-two-year-old resident of Kibera who spent his Sundays not worshipping but attending to his various business interests, these smaller churches were essentially scams. 'In Kibera, a church is a business,' he said, his easy smile tinged with cynicism. He was sitting on a tattered sofa in the shady main room of his mother's house in Kibera, drinking Coke from a glass bottle. 'A church is the easiest way to get money from the aid organisations. One day, you fill up your church with kids – somebody who's dirty, some-body who's not eating – and then the organisation comes and sees the church is full, and they take photos to show their spon-sors, and they give you money.' He chuckled. 'It's all about the photos, you know?'

In another part of Kibera, reached by pursuing still narrower paths, deeper into the slum, then rounding a bend past a health clinic, three Kiberan men were starting their work day at the goat-bone recycling facility. It was an open-air compound, arranged in straightforward fashion: a pile of newly cleaned goat bones on one side, various saws and grinding implements in the middle, and then, on the other side, the results of their labours: beer-bottle openers, necklaces and other trinkets, waiting to be transported to central Nairobi to be sold to tourists. A chunky battery-powered cassette recorder was playing classic rock, though if you listened you could hear singing from the church on the hill. The smell of *nyama choma*, or roasted goat meat, sizzling on an open grill nearby wafted through the workshop, masking the odour of sewage.

Commercially speaking, Sunday in Kibera was no different to any other day, and that meant it was busy. Past the bone workshop, past the street grills, down along an alley covered with blue plastic sheeting, a gateway marked the official entrance to the slum's vast market. But the boundary wasn't obvious, because the whole of Kibera felt like a market. Along every crater-ridden lane, merchants at makeshift tables sold radios, or pineapples, or baby clothes in fluorescent colours; the navigators of wheelbarrows piled with building materials or discarded electronics veered to the left and right to avoid collisions with other people, and other wheelbarrows.

Meanwhile, in an alley leading away from the market, past an establishment showing British Premier League football matches on a satellite television, a man who gave his name as George was at home, working out at the gym he had improvised in his tiny yard. His barbell was a repurposed iron pipe, with concrete poured into cylindrical water vats at each end, in place of weight plates. 'A hundred and fifty kilograms!' he claimed, when asked how much he was hefting above his massive shoulders, making the veins in his forehead pulse. His children craned their necks out from behind the cloth covering their home's main room, and laughed at him.

By the standards of someone from almost anywhere else, the conditions faced by Kibera's residents – who number anywhere from 170,000 to a million, according to competing population surveys – are almost unimaginably harsh. The slum has no running water and no electricity, except what its residents 'borrow' by clipping wires to the cables that run overhead, bringing power to Nairobi's better-off citizens. Sexual violence is rampant. Car-jackings and opportunistic murders are a weekly occurrence. With no proper sanitation, Kibera's primary means of disposing of human waste is what the slum-dwellers wryly refer to as 'flying toilets': the practice of defecating into a plastic bag, then flinging it as far from your own home as possible. Flying toilets add diarrhoea and typhoid fever to the neighbourhood's catalogue of woes, which also includes the fact that, according to some estimates, 20 per cent of the population is infected with HIV.

For all these reasons – and also because it is a conveniently short drive from central Nairobi, with its international airport and comfortable business hotels – Kibera has become a world-famous landmark of suffering. Prime ministers and presidents travel there for photo-opportunities; television news crews come regularly to gawp; and the slum has disproportionately become the focus of hundreds of aid groups, many of them religious, mostly from the United States and Europe. Their names reflect the sense of agonised desperation for which the name 'Kibera' has come to stand: the Fountain of Hope Initiative; Seeds of Hope; Shining Hope for Communities; the Kibera Hope Centre; Kibera in Need.

But ask Norbert Aluku, a lanky young social worker, born and raised in Kibera, if his childhood there was one of misery and suffering, and he will laugh at you in disbelief. 'Of course not! Because, at the end of the day, it's not about your conditions. It's about taking whatever you have and using it as best you can, together with your neighbours. In Kibera, it's only with your neighbours that you're going to get by.' Or ask Irene Mueni, who lives there too, and who speaks darkly of traumatising events in her childhood, yet who still says: 'Happiness is subjective. You can be happy in a slum, unhappy in a city. The things you need for happiness aren't the things you think you need.'

This is the difficult truth that strikes many visitors to Kibera, and they struggle for the words to express it, aware that it is open to misinterpretation. Bluntly, Kiberans just don't seem as unhappy or as depressed as one might have expected. 'It's clear that poverty has crippled Kibera,' observes Jean-Pierre Larroque, a documentary filmmaker who has spent plenty of time there, 'but it doesn't exactly induce the pity-inducing cry for help that NGOs, church missions, and charity groups would have you believe.' What you see instead, he notes, are 'streets bustling with industry'. Kibera feels not so much like a place of despair as a hotbed of entrepreneurialism.

This awkward realisation – that people living in extremely fragile circumstances seem surprisingly high-functioning and non-depressed – isn't applicable only to Kibera, of course. It's so familiar that it has become a cliché, especially regarding sub-Saharan Africa. And it is laden with problems: it coasts close to a number of distasteful generalisations, perhaps even to racism, as well as to poisonous myths about 'primitive' people, uncorrupted by modernity. It can lead to questionable political conclusions, too: if people who are suffering from severe poverty and poor health are so happy, certain commentators are inclined to suggest, perhaps they don't require outside support. And we cringe, surely rightly, when we hear well-heeled celebrities speak in rapt tones about the simple joys of having nothing – as when, for example, Coleen Rooney, television presenter and footballer's wife, told an interviewer: 'I find it so inspiring when you see people from poorer countries on TV: they just seem so happy with their lives, despite their lack of material things . . . in the future, I plan to visit somewhere like Africa.'

The problem with merely dismissing this entire outlook as wrong or misguided, though, is that it appears to be at least partly true. International surveys of happiness – including several reputable research projects such as the World Values Survey – have consistently found some of the world's poorest countries to be among the happiest. (Nigeria, where 92 per cent of the population lives on less than two dollars a day, has come in in first place.) Survey data from the Afrobarometer research project, which monitors more than a dozen African countries, including Kenya, has indicated 'unusual levels of optimism among the poorest and most insecure respondents' in those places. Certain specific measures, such as how optimistic parents feel about their children's futures, actually appear to be *inversely* correlated with wealth and education: the least privileged report feeling the most upbeat. According to mental health researchers, anxiety disorders and depression are far less common in poorer countries. (Their studies take into account the difference in likelihood of getting diagnosed.) In one recent review of mental health problems around the world, sub-Saharan Africa came bottom in terms of prevalence; the top positions were all occupied by richer, industrialised regions.

'Look, this is a thing that social scientists have often pointed out,' Norbert told me when I made my second visit to Kibera. We were sitting on folding chairs in the shade cast by his one-storey office building on the outskirts of the slum. 'Just because you have social problems, it doesn't mean you don't have happiness. Do richer people have fewer problems, really? We have politicians going to jail for corruption, and I really don't think they're happy compared to me. There are problems at every level. Like heart disease or blood pressure if you're stressed.' He shrugged. 'Isn't that obvious?'

This is a psychological phenomenon that stands in need of explanation. Even if there is some debate about the methodologies of international surveys of happiness; even if the impressions of

Jean-Pierre Larroque and others don't capture the whole picture
– why is it that places such as Kibera aren't unequivocally at the
bottom of every assessment of happiness levels every time? A
multiplicity of answers has been advanced, and none of them are
completely satisfying. One is simply that people's expectations
are lower. A related one is based on the (true) observation that
happiness is relative: people who aren't surrounded by examples
of more pleasant lifestyles don't rank their own situation so poorly.
The problem with these arguments is that they all too easily drift
into the condescending suggestion that slum-dwellers don't know
any better – that they are simply unaware that it might be possible
to live with running water, functioning toilets, and lower rates of
disease. But this is certainly not the case in Kibera, whose residents
live shoulder-to-shoulder with Nairobi's fancier neighbourhoods;
some of them have jobs as domestic workers there. The grand
mansion of a senior Kenyan politician sits just a modest walk back
up the road from the slum to Nairobi. In a girls' school in the
heart of Kibera, five-year-olds learn to read beneath a giant photograph of Times Square; Hollywood movies on videotape are
commonplace. Norbert Aluku had even coined a term – 'the thirst'
– for the ambition he tried to instill in younger Kiberans precisely
by taking them to better areas of Nairobi to show them what could
be theirs. Not knowing any better, in this case at least, doesn't
explain the mystery.

I don't have an answer to the puzzle, either. But it does become
a little less mysterious when viewed in the context of the
psychology of security and insecurity. We have seen how pursuing
our desire for a feeling of security can lead us badly astray; and
that vulnerability may be a precondition for the very things that
bring the greatest happiness – strong social relationships above
all. What the people of Kibera and others in similar situations all

share is a lack of access to those things that the rest of us self-defeatingly try to use to quell our feelings of insecurity. The point is certainly not that it's better not to have money, say, than it is to have it. But it's surely undeniable that if you don't have it, it's much harder to overinvest emotionally in it. The same goes for prestigious jobs, material possessions, or impressive educational qualifications: when you have little chance of obtaining them, you won't be misled into thinking they bring more happiness than they do. More broadly, living in such desperate circumstances means that shutting out feelings of insecurity is not a viable option. You have to turn and face the reality of insecurity instead. The people of Kibera are vulnerable whether they like it or not.

One American working in Kibera, Paige Elenson, told me she'd been strongly affected by just this realisation. 'I hate all that romanticism – "Oh, they're so happy,"' she told me. 'In many ways, they're really not . . . but when you don't have access to the good clothes and the nice jobs, when you don't have any of that to hold on to, you have to let people know you through your way of being, not through what you're wearing, or your job title. You actually have to be kind to people if you want them to like you! You have to look into their eyes! We don't have that so much in the US, because it's, like, 'Look what I'm wearing; look what it says on my business card – I don't need to be nice to you'. So there is this vulnerability, which is another way of saying that there's less pretence. I don't know that that makes you happier, necessarily . . . But when there's less to latch onto – when there are choices you don't have – then it changes things. You have to cut the crap.'

Speaking of crap: One day in Kibera, Norbert took me to see a project he was associated with, which involved recycling human waste into marketable biogas. This offered a new solution to the problem of flying toilets. People would stop flinging bags of the stuff into the street, he figured, once they began to realise they could make money from it. It was typical Kiberan pragmatism, assisted in this case by an American aid group. When Norbert talked about the importance of working with your neighbours and of working with what you had, he wasn't speaking in saccharine clichés. The communal activities he was talking about included recycling human waste.

'Look,' said Frankie Oluoch, drinking Coke on his mother's sofa, when I asked him about all this, 'Kibera is not a good place. Big problems, and a million NGOs who don't do any good. Major, major problems. But you have to manage, because you have to. So you take what you have and you get on with it. And you can be happy like that, because happiness comes from your family and other people, and in making something better of yourself, and in new horizons . . . right? Why worry about something you don't have?'

Above all, living in a situation of such inherent insecurity, while very far from preferable, was *clarifying*. Nobody would envy it. But living with fewer illusions meant facing reality head-on. Not having the option of trying to protect yourself in counter-productive ways made for a resilience in the face of hardship that qualified, in the end, as a modest but extremely durable kind of happiness.

We have seen that security may not always be the benefit we imagine it to be, and that insecurity may be compatible with – or perhaps even, in some sense, conducive to – happiness. But an even more radical suggestion is that our search for security might be based on a fundamental misunderstanding – that security, in the famed words of Helen Keller, 'is mostly a superstition'. To understand the enormous implications of this idea, we need to return, a final time, to the work of Alan Watts.

Watts begins his slim 1951 treatise *The Wisdom of Insecurity* by pointing out that there is one overwhelming explanation for his era's feelings of insecurity: the progress of science. Fewer and fewer of us can convince ourselves, if we ever could, that we are headed for an afterlife of eternal bliss; or that there is a God watching out for us; or that the moral rules laid down by the Pope or the Archbishop of Canterbury are unquestionably the ones we ought to follow. 'It is simply self-evident', he writes, 'that during the past century the authority of science has taken the place of the authority of religion in the popular imagination, and that scepticism, at least in spiritual things, has become more general than belief.' Watts, it is true, was writing prior to the resurgence of fundamentalist Christianity in America. But he might well have viewed that development as an inevitable reaction to the very scientific dominance he was describing.

It should go without saying – and Watts very much agrees – that scientific enquiry has brought immeasurable benefits. But at the same time, it has left many feeling a spiritual void. By eliminating gods and the afterlife, the scientific picture of the universe seems to have sapped individual human lives of any special meaning; we fit in only as mere organisms, living out our brief lives for no reason and then perishing. This, he suggests, is the source of the ultimate insecurity, the one that underlies all the others. Yet retreating back under the comforting wing of the old, doctrinaire religions isn't an option for most of us; you can't re-convince yourself of claims that you know are untrue. Are we stuck, then, with the choice of living meaningless but scientifically truthful lives, or lives based on super-stition and self-deception? Watts insists that there is a third alternative, and it's what the rest of his little book is about.

The starting-point for this argument is the observation that impermanence is the nature of the universe: that 'the only constant is change'. It was Heraclitus, living in the fifth and sixth centuries BC, who said that 'no man steps in the same river twice', and his contemporary Confucius, in China, who was supposed to have pointed at a stream and observed, 'It is always flowing, day and night'. People, animals, plants, communities, and civilisations all grow, change, and die: it is the most obvious fact in the world, and almost everybody, scientific or religious, agrees with it.

Yet for all the obviousness of this insight, Watts observes, we seem to live in a constant state of fighting against it, struggling to find security, permanence, fixity, and stability. His point is not to scold you to give up the struggle against impermanence – 'Calling a desire bad names', he writes, 'doesn't get rid of it.' Instead, he wants to make you see that it is an error of a fundamental kind. Attempting to fix change is a contradiction; you can no more fix change than you can make heat cold or green purple. 'There is a contradiction in wanting to be perfectly secure in a universe whose very nature is momentariness and fluidity,' he writes. Even discussing the subject, he points out, risks a similar contradiction, because it is in the nature of language to try to fix and define. And so the most fundamental characteristic of the universe is therefore the one about which it is most difficult to speak.

But it's worse than a mere contradiction – because what we are really doing when we attempt to achieve fixity in the midst of change, Watts argues, is trying to *separate* ourselves from all that change, trying to enforce a distinction between ourselves and the rest of the world. To seek security is to try to remove yourself from change, and thus from the thing that defines life. 'If I want to be secure, that is, protected from the flux of life,' Watts writes,

'I am wanting to be separate from life.' Which brings us to the crux of the matter: it is because we want to feel secure that we build up the fortifications of ego, in order to defend ourselves, but it is those very fortifications that create the feeling of insecurity: 'To be secure means to isolate and fortify the "I", but it is just this feeling of being an isolated "I" which makes me feel lonely and afraid.' This is a strikingly counterintuitive notion: appreciating it entails a mental shift similar to that moment when the famous optical illusion switches from resembling a beautiful young woman to an old witch. We build castle walls to keep out the enemy, but it is the building of the walls that causes the enemy to spring into existence in the first place. It's only because there are castle walls that there is anything to attack. 'The desire for security and the feeling of insecurity are the same thing,' concludes Watts. 'To hold your breath is to lose your breath. A society based on the quest for security is nothing but a breath-retention contest, in which everyone is as taut as a drum and as purple as a beet.' Even if we temporarily and partially achieve the feeling of security, he adds, it doesn't feel good. Life inside the castle walls proves lonely and isolating. 'We discover [not only] that there is no safety, [and] that seeking it is painful, [but] that when we imagine we have found it, we don't like it.'

To understand the final flourish that Watts has in store, think back to the end of the previous chapter, and the challenge it presented to our assumptions about the nature of the self. There, we confronted the fact that there seems to be no straightforward place at which to draw the line between 'self' and 'other' – and that the boundary itself, even if we settle on somewhere to draw it, is more of a meeting point than a dividing line. 'Self' and 'other' rely on each other for their very existence. If that's true, it follows that 'security' is a mistake – because it implies a notion of separate selfhood that doesn't make much sense. What does it even *mean* to separate yourself from an ecosystem that is, in fact, what constitutes you? The point is not to 'confront' insecurity, but to appreciate that *you are it*. Watts writes:

> To understand that there is no security is far more than to agree with the theory that all things change, more even than to observe the transitoriness of life. The notion of security is based on the feeling that there is something within us which is permanent, something which endures through all the days and changes of life. We are struggling to make sure of the permanence, continuity, and safety of this enduring core, this center and soul of our being, which we call 'I'. For this we think to be the real man – the thinker of our thoughts, the feeler of our feelings, the knower of our knowledge. We do not actually understand that there is no security until we realize that this 'I' does not exist.

This extraordinary passage, once you grasp the point – and it took me a while – explains in the most complete sense why our efforts to find happiness are so frequently sabotaged by 'ironic' effects, delivering the exact opposite of what we set out to gain. All positive thinking, all goalsetting and visualising and looking on the bright side, all trying to make things *go our way*, as opposed to some other way, is rooted in an assumption about the separateness of 'us' and those 'things'. But on closer inspection this assumption collapses. Trying to flee from insecurity to security, from uncertainty to certainty, is an attempt to find an exit from the very system that makes us who we are in the first place. We can influence the system of which we are a part, certainly. But if we are motivated by this misunderstanding about who we are, and what security is, we'll always risk going too far, trying too hard, in self-defeating ways. Watts concludes:

> The real reason why human life can be so utterly exasperating and frustrating is not because there are facts called death, pain, fear, or hunger. The madness of the thing is that when such facts are present, we circle, buzz, writhe, and whirl, trying to get the 'I' out of the experience . . . Sanity, wholeness and integration lie in the realization that we are not divided, that man and his present experience are one, and that no separate 'I' or mind can be found . . . [Life] is a dance, and when you are dancing, you are not intent on getting somewhere. The meaning and purpose of dancing is the dance.

This, then, is the deep truth about insecurity: it is another word for life. That doesn't mean it's not wise to protect yourself, as far as you can, from certain specific dangers. But it does mean that feeling secure and really living life are, in some ultimate sense, opposites. And that you can no more succeed in achieving perfect security than a wave could succeed in leaving the ocean.

7

The Museum of Failure

The Case for Embracing Your Errors

You can't turn a sow's ear into a Veal Orloff. But you can do something very good with a sow's ear.

— Julia Child

IN AN UNREMARKABLE BUSINESS park near the airport outside the city of Ann Arbor, in Michigan, stands a poignant memorial to humanity's shattered dreams. Not that you'd know it from the outside. From the outside, it looks like a car dealership, because that's what it was until 2001, when a company with the enigmatic name of GfK Custom Research North America moved in. Even when you get inside – which members of the public rarely do – it takes a few moments for your eyes to adjust to what you're seeing. There is no lobby or reception desk, no list of departments, nobody waiting to greet you. Instead, you find yourself in what appears to be a vast and haphazardly organised supermarket. It contains no shoppers, but along every aisle the grey metal shelves are crammed with tens of thousands of packages of food and household products. There is something unusually cacophonous about these displays, and soon enough, you work out the reason.

Unlike in a real supermarket, there is only one of each item; there are no uniform ranks of jars of pasta sauce, boxes of dishwasher detergent, or fizzy-drink cans. The more important point about the products on these shelves, though, is that many of them would be impossible to find in a real supermarket anyway. They are failures: products withdrawn from sale after a few weeks or months because almost nobody wanted to buy them. In the product-design business, GfK Custom Research's storehouse of fiascos has acquired the nickname of 'the museum of failed products'. It is consumer capitalism's graveyard – the shadow side to the relentlessly upbeat, success-focused culture of modern marketing. Or to put it less grandly: it's almost certainly the only place on the planet where you'll find Clairol's Touch of Yogurt shampoo, alongside Gillette's equally unpopular For Oily Hair Only, a few feet from a now-empty bottle of Pepsi A.M. Breakfast Cola (born 1989; died 1990). The museum is home to discontinued brands of caffeinated beer; to TV dinners branded with the logo of the toothpaste manufacturer Colgate; to self-heating soup cans that had a regrettable tendency to explode in customers' faces; and to packets of breath mints that had to be withdrawn from sale because they looked like the tiny packages of crack cocaine dispensed by America's street dealers. It is where microwavable scrambled eggs – pre-scrambled and packaged in a cardboard tube, with a pop-up mechanism for easier consumption in the car – go to die.

Laugh too hard at any of these products, though, and the museum's proprietor, an understatedly stylish GfK employee named Carol Sherry, will purse her lips and arch her eyebrows over her Dolce & Gabbana spectacles as if to chide you. And she will be only half joking. It is Sherry's job to act as chaperone to the product designers and other executives who pay significant sums for the right to inspect GfK's collection, and she treats the products in her care like disappointing yet still fundamentally lovable children. One bright December morning, giving me a tour of the building, she paused before a cream-coloured bottle of body lotion, and an expression close to sadness flickered across her face. 'Ah, yes, now, this,' she said fondly. 'Pulled very abruptly from the market. Unfortunately, it led to an increased risk of fungal infection.'

There is a Japanese term, *mono no aware*, that translates very roughly as 'the pathos of things'. It captures a kind of poignant melancholy at life's impermanence – that additional beauty imparted to cherry blossoms, or cloud formations, or human features, as a result of their inevitably fleeting time on earth. It is only stretching this concept slightly to suggest that Sherry feels the same way about, for example, the cartons of Morning Banana Juice in her care, or about Fortune Snookies, a short-lived line of fortune cookies for dogs. Every failure, the way she sees it, embodies its own sad story of sincere effort on the part of designers, marketers, salespeople and others. It is never far from her mind that real people had their mortgages, their car payments, and their family holidays riding on the success of Touch of Yogurt or Fortune Snookies. Or of Heublein Wine & Dine Dinners, a line of pre-prepared meals packaged with a half-sized bottle of cooking wine, which customers, understandably, assumed was meant for drinking. (Then they tasted the wine. And then they stopped buying Heublein Wine & Dine Dinners.)

'I feel really sorry for the developer on this one,' Sherry said, indicating the breath mints that inadvertently resembled crack. 'I mean, I've met the guy. Why would he ever have spent any time on the streets, in the drug culture? He did everything right, except go out on the streets to see if his product looked like drugs.' She shook her head. 'To me, it takes incredible courage to be a product developer. There are so many ways it could go wrong. These are real people, who get up every morning and sincerely want to do their best, and then, well . . . things happen.'

The museum of failed products was itself a kind of accident, albeit a happier one. Its creator, a now-retired marketing man named Robert McMath, merely intended to accumulate a 'reference library' of consumer products, not failures per se. Starting in the 1960s, he began purchasing and preserving a sample of every new item he could find. (He usually emptied out any perishable contents, to stop things getting disgusting.) Soon the collection outgrew his office in upstate New York and he was forced to move into a converted granary to accommodate it. Later, GfK – the initials are derived from the German name of its parent company – bought him out, moving the whole lot to Michigan. What McMath hadn't taken into account, he told me on the phone from his home in California, was the three-word truth that was to prove the making of his career: 'Most products fail.' According to some estimates, the failure rate is as high as 90 per cent. Simply by collecting new products indiscriminately, McMath had ensured that his hoard would come to consist overwhelmingly of unsuccessful ones. 'You know, I never really liked the term "museum of failed products",' he told me. 'But there it is. It stuck. There wasn't much I could do about it.'

I suspected him of being a little disingenuous about this, since all the evidence suggests that McMath revelled in his reputation as a guru of failure. In the early years, he was a fixture on the lecture circuit, and then on American cable television; David Letterman even interviewed him about what McMath was happy to refer to as his 'library of losers'. He wrote a marketing manual, *What Were They Thinking?*, devoted largely to poking fun at products such as Revlon's No Sweat antiperspirant and Look of

Buttermilk, a companion product to Clairol's Touch of Yogurt. (As McMath points out, you should never mention sweat when marketing anti-sweat products, because shoppers find it repulsive. It's entirely unclear, meanwhile, what the 'look of buttermilk' might be, let alone why you might wish your hair to sport it.) But Sherry seemed disapproving of the levity with which her predecessor had approached his work. 'Originally, yes, the hook with the media was that he was the owner of a museum of failures,' she sighed. 'But I think that's just a shame. It's human to point fingers and revel in someone else's misery, I guess. But I just feel very attached to everything in here.' She had a point. True, I laughed when I encountered Goff's Low Ash Cat Food, with its proud boast, 'contains only one point five per cent ash!' (As the journalist Neil Steinberg has noted, this is like marketing a line of hot dogs called Few Mouse Hairs.) Yet several people presumably invested months of their lives in creating that cat food. I hope they can look back and chuckle about it now. But who knows?

By far the most striking thing about the museum of failed products, though, has to do with the fact that it exists as a viable, profit-making business in the first place. You might have assumed that any consumer product manufacturer worthy of the name would have its own such collection, a carefully stewarded resource to help it avoid repeating errors its rivals had already made. Yet the executives arriving every week at Carol Sherry's door are evidence of how rarely this happens. Product developers are so focused on their next hoped-for success – and so unwilling to invest time or energy in thinking about their industry's past failures – that they only belatedly realise how much they need, and are willing to pay, to access GfK's collection. Most surprising of all is the fact that many of the designers who have found their way to the museum

of failed products, over the years, have come there in order
to examine – or, alternatively, have been surprised to discover –
products that *their own companies* had created and then abandoned.
These firms were apparently so averse to thinking about the
unpleasant business of failure that they had neglected even to keep
samples of their own disasters.

'Here's how it usually goes,' said McMath. 'A product will be
developed by a product manager, and it won't work out, and he'll
probably just keep a few in his bedroom closet, for sentimental
value, but then he'll eventually leave the company.' The product
may now no longer exist anywhere, except in the manager's
bedroom. Nor, of course, will he bring examples of his failures
to his next place of work: why voluntarily associate yourself with
misfires? 'People are inspired by success and achievement, and
marketing people are as human as anyone,' said Sherry. 'You want
to be able to tell a good story about your accomplishments.' It is
unlikely that many people at his former firm will want to dwell
on what went wrong, either. Failure simply isn't a topic on which
ambitious people wish to spend much of their time. At best, it's
just depressing; at worst, it feels somehow infectious – as if the
germs of disaster might infect your next project. Recall the message
of Dr Robert H. Schuller, at Get Motivated!, instructing his audience to cut the word 'impossible' out of their vocabularies and
to refuse to contemplate the possibility of failure. The very fact
that the consumer products industry needs a museum of failed
products indicates that many product designers and marketing
executives have done exactly that.

McMath turned a little coy when I asked him to tell me which
executives, specifically, had found themselves compelled to visit
his collection, tails between legs, to examine their own companies'
products, though after some pestering he let it be known that

some of them might have worked for a multinational beginning with 'P' and ending in 'rocter & Gamble'. But he did vividly remember one product design team who approached him with a plan to market two companion lines of sex-specific diapers, for boys and girls, with the padding configured differently in each. This turns out to have been an often-attempted, often-abandoned innovation: parents generally don't see the need, while retailers resent having to use up more shelf space in order to avoid running out of either kind. It was with glee that Robert McMath ushered the designers to an aisle in his collection to show them not only that their idea had already been tried – but that it had been their own firm that had tried it.

Failure is everywhere. It's just that most of the time we would rather avoid confronting that fact.

Failure, and our fraught relationship to it, is a theme that has been playing in the background of much of this book so far. It is the thing that the culture of positive thinking strives at all costs to avoid, so it should come as little surprise that it should be so central to an alternative approach to happiness. The Stoic technique of negative visualisation is, precisely, about turning towards the possibility of failure. The critics of goalsetting are effectively proposing a new attitude towards failure, too, since an improvisational, trial-and-error approach necessarily entails being frequently willing to fail. The spiritual ruminations of Eckhart Tolle and Alan Watts, meanwhile, point to an even deeper kind of failure: the ultimate – and ultimately liberating – failure of the ego's efforts to maintain its separation and security.

But it is also worth considering the subject of failure directly, in order to see how the desperate efforts of the 'cult of optimism' to avoid it are so often counterproductive, and how we might be better off learning to embrace it. The first reason to turn towards failure is that our efforts not to think about failure leave us with a severely distorted understanding of what it takes to be successful. The second is that an openness to the emotional experience of failure can be a stepping-stone to a much richer kind of happiness than can be achieved by focusing only on success. It has become fashionable, in some circles, to insist upon the importance of 'embracing failure': no autobiography of a high-profile entrepreneur or politician or inventor is complete without several passages in which the author attributes his or her success to a willingness to fail. (Sir Richard Branson is a repeat offender in this regard.) But truly embracing failure entails a shift in perspective far greater than what most such figures mean when they pay lip-service to the notion. And in any case, heeding only the advice of the successful is a big part of the problem.

Our resistance to thinking about failure is especially curious in light of the fact that failure is so ubiquitous. 'Failure is the distinguishing feature of corporate life,' writes the economist Paul Ormerod, at the start of his book *Why Most Things Fail*, but in this sense corporate life is merely a microcosm of the whole of life. Evolution itself is driven by failure; we think of it as a matter of survival and adaptation, but it makes equal sense to think of it as a matter of not surviving and not adapting. Or perhaps more sense: of all the species that have ever existed, after all, fewer than 1 per cent of them survive today. The others failed. On an individual level, too, no matter how much success you may experience in life, your eventual story – no offence intended – will be one of failure. Your bodily organs will fail, and you'll die.

Yet though failure is ubiquitous, psychologists have long recognised that we find this notion appalling, and that we will go to enormous lengths to avoid thinking about it. At its pathological extreme, this fear of failure is known as 'kakorrhaphiophobia', the symptoms of which can include heart palpitations, hyperventilation and dizziness. Few of us suffer so acutely. But as we'll see, this may only be because we are so naturally skilled at 'editing out' our failures, in order to retain a memory of our actions that is vastly more flattering than the reality. Like product managers with failures stuffed into a bedroom closet, we will do anything to tell a success-based story of our lives. This leads, among other consequences, to the entertaining psychological phenomenon known as 'illusory superiority'. This mental glitch explains why, for example, the vast majority of people tell researchers that they consider themselves to be in the top 50 per cent of safe drivers – even though they couldn't possibly all be.

Like many commentators concerned about our reluctance to confront failure, Robert McMath likes to argue that we should behave 'more like scientists'. The implication is that scientists, unlike the rest of us, must by necessity learn to become more comfortable with failure. Professional scientists, not surprisingly, tend to share this flattering view. The goal of every good scientist is discovering the truth, so he can't be picky about whether the results of his experiments confirm or undermine his hypotheses. Scientific research involves devising a hypothesis, testing it, and then dealing with whatever results you obtain – even if they ruin your hopes of a prize-winning breakthrough. Right? Actually, maybe not. A fascinating series of studies of working scientists, conducted by the Irish-born researcher Kevin Dunbar, presents a very different picture – and confirms just how deeply and universally human the tendency to avoid confronting failure really is. Scientists, it transpires, may be just as bad as everyone else.

Dunbar negotiated access to four leading molecular biology

laboratories and began observing the work that was conducted there. For months, he videotaped interviews and recorded the weekly lab meetings at which researchers discussed their findings. (This kind of examination of what scientists do on a day-to-day basis is rare, not least because scientists themselves frequently dismiss it as irrelevant.) Dunbar's first discovery was that the researchers encountered failure all the time. 'If you're a scientist and you're doing an experiment,' he said later, 'about half the experiments that you do actually turn out wrong.' For whatever reason – faulty procedures or a flawed hypothesis – the results obtained did not mesh with the conclusions towards which the scientists believed they were advancing. As one of Dunbar's subjects put it in a meeting, describing yet another failure: 'I saw the results, and I wanted to throw myself off a bridge.'

Things got more interesting when Dunbar examined how the researchers responded to this deluge of failure. As he explained in an interview with *Wired* magazine, their reactions followed a predictable sequence. First, a scientist would blame his equipment or techniques – suspecting that a measuring device must be malfunctioning, or that he himself had made a stupid mistake. If the problem couldn't be explained away so easily, the researcher would then repeat the experiment, sometimes several times, in hopes that the anomaly would vanish. And if that didn't work, he would often simply put the experiment aside. Laboratories are busy places; scientists are overworked; there are vastly more potential avenues for research than could ever be pursued, and so researchers have to make choices about what they will focus on next. Consistently, Kevin Dunbar found, they chose to neglect their inexplicable results, focusing on their successes and avoiding dwelling upon their failures.

Using brain imaging, Dunbar has examined the part of the

human brain that seems most implicated in screening out failure: the dorsolateral prefrontal cortex, or DLPFC. This region plays a crucial role in filtering out irrelevant or unwanted incoming information, which is essential if you want to concentrate, say, on a single conversation at a noisy cocktail party. (People with damaged DLPFCs experience difficulty with such tasks.) But a similar filtering process appears to be triggered when we are presented with information that violates our expectations, even when it is far from irrelevant. In one experiment, Dunbar showed videos to an audience of physics students in which two objects of different sizes, dropped from the top of a tower, appeared to behave in defiance of the laws of gravity: they fell at different speeds. Physics students know that's not what really happens, and their DLPFCs lit up – much more so than was the case in viewers of the videos who weren't so familiar with this law of physics. Dunbar's hunch is that the physics students' brains were reacting to the unwanted, clearly inexplicable information by attempting to delete it from their awareness.

Back in Ann Arbor, at the museum of failed products, it wasn't hard to imagine how a similar aversion to confronting failure might have been responsible for the very existence of many of the products lining its shelves. Each one must have made it through a series of meetings at which nobody realised that the product was doomed. Perhaps nobody wanted to contemplate the prospect of failure; perhaps someone did, but didn't want to bring it up for discussion. Even if the product's likely failure was recognised, Robert McMath explained, those responsible for marketing it might well have responded by ploughing *more* money into it. This is a common reaction when a product looks like it's going to be a lemon, since with a big enough marketing spend, a marketing manager can at least guarantee a few sales, sparing the company total humiliation. By the time reality sets in, McMath notes in *What Were They Thinking?*, it is quite possible that 'the executives will have been promoted to another brand, or recruited by another company'. Thanks to a collective unwillingness to face up to failure, more money will have been invested in the doomed product, and little energy will have been dedicated to examining what went wrong. Everyone involved will have conspired – perhaps without realising what they're doing – never to think or speak of it again.

The first big problem with our reluctance to think about or analyse failure – whether our own or other people's – is that it leads to an utterly distorted picture of the causes of success. Some years ago, a management theorist from Oxford University named Jerker Denrell was attending an academic conference in Stockholm, in his native Sweden, and sitting through the kind of speech that can make it hard to stay awake. Up at the podium, a fellow researcher was explaining his findings about the personality traits of highly successful entrepreneurs. According to several new case studies, the speaker announced, high achievers demonstrated two key characteristics: they were willing to persevere in the face of setbacks, and they possessed enough charisma to convince others to follow them. All of which is boringly obvious, and it is easy to imagine eyelids across the conference hall beginning to droop. But Denrell found himself paying attention. The speech he was hearing, he realised, embodied an error that he had been encountering for some time; he had just never heard it so clearly expressed. It was a mistake so basic that it threatened to undermine a large proportion of his colleagues' work.

It may well be true that successful entrepreneurs possess

perseverance and leadership skills, of course. What is less obvious – and much less boring – is what the speaker neglected to mention: that those traits are likely to be the characteristics of extremely *unsuccessful* people, too. 'Think about it,' Denrell observed afterwards. 'Incurring large losses requires both persistence . . . and the ability to persuade others to pour their money down the drain.' People without much perseverance or charisma are more likely to end up in the middle, experiencing neither great success nor great failure. (If you never stick at anything and if you can't persuade others to follow you, you may never lead an army of like-minded souls to a stunning victory – but neither will you lead them off a cliff.) It seems entirely likely that the very successful and the very unsuccessful might actually have rather similar personalities. The only indisputable difference between the two is that the very unsuccessful are much, much less frequently interviewed by management scholars who are studying the causes of success. They are, after all, failures. Even if researchers *wanted* to interview them – which, by and large, they don't – it is hard to imagine how they might track them down in significant numbers. Success happens in public; indeed, achieving celebrity is part of many people's definition of what constitutes success. Failure is occasionally spectacular at first, but people who fail dwell largely in obscurity.

This problem, which is known as 'survivor bias' or the 'under-sampling of failure', is already extremely familiar in many areas of scholarship and of life. Most of us grasp it intuitively in certain contexts, of which the canonical example is gambling. We know, deep down, not to conclude that if we have enjoyed a winning streak at the roulette table, we must possess some magical ability to predict the behaviour of the roulette wheel. We understand that winning at roulette is a matter of chance, and that probability dictates that winning streaks will sometimes occur. Losing streaks are more common, of course. It's just that they don't tend to cause any intrigued whispering around the casino. You never hear about all the men and women who *didn't* break the bank at Monte Carlo.

The speech that Jerker Denrell heard in Stockholm was one glaring example of how our conversations about success are always falling foul of the undersampling of failure. But there are countless others. Take the bestselling book *The Millionaire Next Door*, by the American researcher Thomas Stanley. This purports to be a research-based portrait of the millionaire personality, and though the jacket describes its conclusions as 'surprising', they really aren't. The typical millionaire, Stanley reveals, is disciplined and driven, street-smart but not necessarily intellectual, and frugal to the point of tight-fistedness. *The Millionaire Next Door*, its publishers claim, 'shattered one of contemporary America's most firmly held myths: that wealthy individuals belong to an elite group of the highly educated and exceedingly lucky, who often inherit their money and spend it on lavish purchases and pampered lifestyles'. The implication throughout – and surely the explanation for the book's commercial success – is that if you, too, were to become self-disciplined, street-smart and frugal, you too could make a million. Except that, knowing what we know about survivor bias, that doesn't necessarily follow at all. Judging by his own account of his research, Stanley spent no time whatsoever studying the personalities of those who had tried but failed to become millionaires, or those to whom the notion had never occurred. (To be fair, he does mention people who made a fortune but didn't manage to hold on to their money.) And so he has few grounds for concluding that frugality or self-discipline – or any other trait, for that matter – is part of the recipe for becoming a millionaire. Others who were equally frugal or self-disciplined might have come nowhere near millionairehood.

'Suppose you look at successful chief executives and you find they all brush their teeth,' Denrell told me. 'Well, you realise that this isn't a thing unique to chief executives, because everybody brushes their teeth. You know this, because you brush your teeth, too. So you dismiss it. But say they have some strange trait that you don't have much experience of. Well, it will seem to you that this is something that explains their success. It seems to make sense, after all.' And it feels intuitively right to be focusing on the successful, not on the failures: 'If you want to learn how to fly, you look at birds; you don't look at cockroaches.' But focusing solely on success leads us badly astray.

One of the more peculiar consequences of the survivor bias is the way that it casts doubt not only on the work of scholars who study success, but on the explanations that successful people themselves give – and may sincerely believe – for their own achievements. Bookshops are stuffed with autobiographical volumes of advice such as the one released in 2006 by the multi-millionaire publisher Felix Dennis, entitled *How to Get Rich: The Distilled Wisdom of One of Britain's Wealthiest Self-Made Entrepreneurs*. Dennis's book is far less annoying than most such works, thanks largely to his disarming sense of humour about being worth £700 million, and his refreshing honesty about how much he enjoys the yachts and Caribbean holidays and Michelin-starred food that his lifestyle affords him. And yet, beneath the bragging, his book conveys a similar message to many of the others: to make a fortune, you need stubbornness, a lack of regard for what other people think of you, and a willingness to take risks. Those qualities, Dennis suggests, made him what he is. To which Jerker Denrell might respond: how could he possibly know? Dennis, obviously, has lived only one life, and has no experience of an alternative one, culminating in financial failure, with which to compare it. Perhaps thousands of others exhibited the same determination, cheekiness, and pluck, but got nowhere. Maybe not. Maybe Dennis's ascent was due to dumb luck, or to some other personality trait, so that he actually succeeded in spite of his stubbornness or fondness for risks. His self-diagnosis may be correct, of course; it's just that he isn't automatically in a better position than anyone else to say.

Dennis's focus on risk-taking raises an intriguing additional point, which is that the willingness to fail is *itself* one of the personality traits we may come to overvalue as a result of survivor bias. This is the problem with homilies such as those of Richard Branson, who writes: 'Being unafraid of failure is, I believe, one of the most important qualities of a champion.' He may be right about the importance of not fearing failure, but then again, you don't hear speeches or read autobiographies by people who were unafraid of failure and then did indeed simply fail. A willingness to fail might not be associated with success at all; alternatively, as Denrell points out, a willingness to court failure by taking big risks might be correlated with both great success and great failure. The definition of a 'big risk', after all, is that it carries a significant likelihood of things not working out.

A parallel insight arises from Denrell's research into media commentators who make predictions about the future course of the economy. The ones who made the most extreme, headline-grabbing predictions, Denrell and his colleague Christina Fang concluded, were just as likely to prove astonishingly wrong as astonishingly right. They weren't better forecasters; they just made riskier forecasts – while the media, which trumpeted their predictions and praised them when they were vindicated by events, rarely followed up on their failed forecasts. This is something you might wish to consider before relying on such commentators when choosing where to invest your money.

It is worth bearing in mind, moreover, that virtually any advice about how to succeed, in life or work, is at constant risk of being undermined by survivor bias. We ignore or avoid failure so habitually that we rarely stop to consider all the people who may have followed any set of instructions for happiness or success – including those advanced in these pages – but then failed to achieve the result.

This is probably as good a time as any to tell you about my pubic louse.

I acquired the louse – just the one, though it was exceptionally large – in February 2001, at Greenwich in east London, at the site of the Millennium Dome, Britain's fabled monument to the dawn of the year 2000. The story of the dome is, notoriously, one of failure after failure: a financial catastrophe, a disaster in terms of visitor numbers, and the undoing of several prominent politicians' careers. By early 2001, the Millennium Experience, the exhibition that had occupied the interior of the 365-metre-wide marquee for the previous year, had ended. I had been sent, as a newspaper reporter, to witness the auction of the dome's contents, by means of which its now-bankrupt operators hoped to recover some fraction of their lost millions. I had been given £100 of my employer's petty cash, in order to make a purchase for the purposes of entertaining journalism. The serious money, it was clear, was going to be spent on the company's computers, its high-tech lighting rigs and catering equipment, but everything was up for grabs – including the exhibits that had dominated the Dome's fourteen 'zones', dedicated to such topics as Body, Mind, Faith, Work, Money and Play. The Body Zone was a giant replica of a human body – bigger, we had often been told, than the Statue of Liberty – through which visitors (although not enough of them) had walked. Demonstrating an audacious refusal to flinch from the unpalatable realities of their subject, the body's designers had equipped it with several mechanised pubic lice. With my £100, I bought one. The others went to an antiques dealer from Surrey, who told me he planned to use them to scare his wife and children. A man must have a hobby.

A dome employee named Geoff came to help me extract my louse from the storeroom. 'It's a bit sad, really,' he said, with what seemed to be real emotion. 'I used to work with this guy.' I took the creature to the processing desk, as required, where another worker took it from me and handed me a slip of paper. I wouldn't be able to take it off the premises, she explained, until the auction was completed, in a few days' time. Rules were rules.

I returned to the office, louseless and in a reflective mood. The auction had felt like a public admission of the dome's defeat, and thus an appropriate end to the whole saga: sad, but also funny, and above all fitting. The sorry story of the dome is probably best encapsulated by Dan Howland, an expert on fairgrounds and amusement parks, who expresses it as follows in a monograph entitled *Dome and Domer*:

From the moment it opened, it was clear that the Millennium Dome would be one of the grandest and most spectacular failures in exposition history. It was unpopular with both press and public, inaccessible, ill-conceived, poorly planned, mismanaged, and just generally dull. So much money was spent on the dome, and so much more shovelled in as the debacle continued, that Labour prime minister Tony Blair found his career hanging in the balance, while other Labour officials found their careers hanging in tatters. The story of the Millennium Dome is a tale of honest mistakes, bad design, hubris, stupidity, greed, corruption – but above all, it's a tale of something so monumentally awful that it takes on a sort of soggy grandeur.

There is no need to rehearse each of these missteps here. Among the more famous lowlights were the New Year's Eve 1999 opening ceremony, when thousands of invited guests, including influential politicians and national newspaper editors, were forced to shiver outdoors for hours before being funnelled through the dome's hopelessly inadequate number of metal detectors; the bomb threat that almost forced the building's evacuation that night; and the attempted heist, later that year, during which a team of thieves smashed their way inside with a digger and got halfway through executing the robbery of the world's second-largest flawless diamond, which they believed was inside. (Technically, this may not count as a low point for the dome, since the heist was thwarted; an informant had alerted the police, who had replaced the diamond with a replica, and were lying in wait.) The problems had started much earlier, though: in the years approaching the Millennium, many of the project's senior employees and consultants had resigned, and several chief executives had been fired. One of them subsequently told a parliamentary committee that the dome's highest-level staff had been on the verge of nervous breakdowns as 2000 approached, forcing him to hire a team of counsellors. The dome was so vast, we'd been informed, that it could hold 18,000 double-decker London buses. But the consensus among commentators seemed to be that ordering a large quantity of double-decker buses might have been a much better use of the more than £800 million that the project swallowed up.

The Millennium Dome, in other words, could hardly have been more of a catastrophe. And yet it also illustrated the extraordinary power of failure to bring people closer together. The atmosphere at the auction was surprisingly convivial – reflecting not just the schadenfreude of journalists, but an attitude that seemed to have accompanied the tale of the dome from the very beginning: a sort of affectionate popular embrace of the endeavour in all its haplessness. 'It's a souvenir of a national disaster,' one attendee at the auction told me, explaining his presence there. 'It's a very British thing to do, isn't it?' In the months following the auction, as politicians and commentators debated what should become of the now-empty dome, the columnist Ros Coward ably captured this bittersweet British fondness for its failure. This was not joy at the misfortune of others so much as a perverse pride in belonging to the nation whose failure the dome had been:

> The dome has a clear brand, and that brand is Disaster. It cries out to be exploited as a grand folly, an emblem of muddle, hype and plain foolishness with enormous entertainment potential . . . We've become fond of the building we love to hate, the great folly, with all the entertainment it has provided stumbling from crisis to disaster . . . Something about it chimes with the British character. We're good at disasters, at not taking ourselves seriously and delighting when things go magnificently and foolishly wrong . . . This is the key to its future. It should become a museum of disasters and follies, a history of doomed projects or unfortunate accidents.

That never happened, of course. These days, the dome is the O2 arena, a concert venue that occasionally plays host to stadium-sized motivational seminars.

A few days after the auction, I returned to Greenwich to collect my pubic louse, but it was nowhere to be found. The dome employee who helped me look for it was apologetic, but not surprised. Even in attempting to sell off its contents, the dome proved a failure. Over the next few years, I received sporadic letters from the accountants PricewaterhouseCoopers, who were handling the bankruptcy, implying that one day – presumably after more important creditors had been recompensed – I might get my newspaper's £100 back.

I'm still waiting.

This half-embrace of failure, as Coward suggests, is something the British like to think of as distinctly British. We celebrate Captain Scott's failed and fatal effort to be first to the South Pole; we cherish the spirit of the Dunkirk evacuation more than the triumph of victory. 'To all those who have written terrible books on success,' wrote the (British) journalist Stephen Pile in his 1979 bestseller (in Britain) *The Book of Heroic Failures*, 'I dedicate this terrible book on how it's perfectly all right to be incompetent . . . because I am, and so is everyone I know.' To citizens of the success-oriented United States, the fondness for failure can seem like a more generally European eccentricity, frequently attributed to the end of empire. 'Musing over failure is not a particularly American activity,' writes the journalist Neil Steinberg. 'Sure, it's big in Europe, where every nation, at one time or another, has had a lock on greatness, only to fritter it away smothering monster palaces in gold leaf and commissioning jeweled Fabergé eggs by the dozen. England had her empire; Spain, her Armada; France, her Napoleon; Germany, its unspeakable zenith. Even Belgium had a moment of glory – though, true, things haven't been quite the same since the death of Charles the Bold in 1477. For those nations, remembering and bitterly analyzing greatness are [just] about their only connection to it anymore. Why do you think they have all those pubs and outdoor cafés?'

But we should not write off the embrace of failure as a culturally specific quirk; in the context of the 'negative path' to happiness, there is more to say. We have seen already how a willingness to fail and to analyse past failures can be crucial to understanding achievement and success. But a more deeply counterintuitive possibility is that there is happiness to be found in embracing failure *as* failure, not just as a path to success – that welcoming it might simply feel better than perpetually struggling to avoid it.

There is an openness and honesty in failure, a down-to-earth confrontation with reality that is lacking at the higher altitudes of success. To achieve something impressive – as might have happened had the dome ever become, as Tony Blair predicted, 'a beacon to the world' – is necessarily to erect a kind of barrier between yourself and everyone else. To be impressed by something, meanwhile, implies feeling yourself to be in the presence of something different from, and better than, yourself. Failure, by contrast, collapses these boundaries, demonstrating the fallibility of those who might otherwise try to present themselves as immune to defeat. It cuts people down to human size. The vulnerability revealed by failure can nurture empathy and communality. Do you feel more or less connection to the people who ran the dome to learn that they had been on the brink of emotional collapse? The answer, surely, is more. Had the dome been a triumphant success, it would have been unthinkable for a reporter to have had the conversations I found myself having with its employees, who would have been uptight and wary, instructed not to communicate with the media except in ways that might burnish the brand. 'Psychologically, I suppose, it's healthy,' said one security guard, who was keeping watch over four life-sized mannequins in surgical dress that would eventually sell for £320. 'We've come to the funeral, we've buried the body, and we're grieving.' Failure is a relief. At last you can say what you think.

Still, it can be exceptionally hard to adopt this attitude towards your own failures. As Christopher Kayes's notion of 'goalodicy' suggests, we too often make our goals into parts of our identities, so that failure becomes an attack on who we are. Or, as Albert Ellis understood, we alight upon some desired outcome – being happily married, for example, or finding fulfilling work – and elevate it into one we feel we *must* attain, so that failing at it becomes not just sad but catastrophic. To use the Buddhist language of attach-ment and non-attachment, we become attached to success.

All these counterproductive ways of thinking about failure manifest themselves most acutely in the phenomenon of perfec-tionism. This is one of those traits that many people seem secretly, or not so secretly, proud to possess, since it hardly seems like a character flaw – yet perfectionism, at bottom, is a fear-driven striving to avoid the experience of failure at all costs. At its extremes, it is an exhausting and permanently stressful way to live. (There is a greater correlation between perfectionism and suicide, research suggests, than between feelings of hopelessness and suicide.) To fully embrace the experience of failure, not merely to tolerate it as a stepping-stone to success, is to abandon this constant straining never to put a foot wrong. It is to relax. 'Downfall', writes the American Zen Buddhist Natalie Goldberg, 'brings us to the ground, facing the nitty-gritty, things as they are with no glitter. Success cannot last forever. Everyone's time runs out.' She goes on: 'Achievement solidifies us. Believing we are invincible, we want more and more.' To see and feel things as they really are, 'we have to crash. Only then can we drop through to a more authentic self. Zen transmits its legacy from this deeper place. It is a different kind of failure: the Great Failure, a boundless surrender. Nothing to hold on to, and nothing to lose.'

Fortunately, it may be possible to cultivate some of this attitude towards failure without reaching the rarefied heights of Buddhist enlightenment. The work of the Stanford University psychologist Carol Dweck suggests that our experiences of failure are influenced overwhelmingly by the implicit beliefs we hold about the nature of talent and ability – and that we can, perhaps quite easily, nudge ourselves in the direction of a more healthy outlook.

Each of us can be placed somewhere on a continuum, Dweck argues, depending on our 'implicit view' – or unspoken attitude – about what talent is and where it comes from. Those with a 'fixed theory' assume that ability is innate; those with an 'incremental theory' believe that it evolves through challenge and hard work. If you're the kind of person who struggles mightily to avoid the experience of failure, it's likely that you reside near the 'fixed' end of Dweck's continuum. 'Fixed theory' people tend to approach challenges as occasions on which they are called upon to demonstrate their innate abilities, and so they find failure especially horrifying: to them, it's a sign that they tried to show how good they were, but didn't measure up. The classic example of a person with a 'fixed theory' is the young sports star who is encouraged to think of himself as a 'natural' – but who then fails to put in sufficient practice to realise his potential. If talent is innate, his unspoken reasoning goes, then why bother?

'Incremental theory' people are different. Because they think of abilities as emerging through tackling challenges, the experience of failure has a completely different meaning for them: it's evidence that they are stretching themselves to their current limit. If they weren't, they wouldn't fail. The relevant analogy here is with weight training; muscles grow by being pushed to the limits of their current capacity, where fibres tear and reheal. Among weightlifters, 'training to failure' isn't an admission of defeat – it's a strategy.

Happily, Dweck's studies indicate that we are not saddled for life with one mindset rather than another. A little confusingly, the 'fixed' mindset is not itself fixed, but can be shifted towards the 'incremental' end of the continuum. Some people manage to alter their outlook simply by being introduced to the 'fixed' versus 'incremental' distinction. Alternatively, it's worth trying to recall it when failure strikes: next time you flunk an exam or mishandle a social situation, consider that it is happening only because you're pushing at the limits of your present abilities – and therefore, over the long run, improving them. Should you wish to encourage an incremental outlook rather than a fixed one in your children, Dweck advises, take care to praise them for their effort rather than for their intelligence. Focusing on the latter is likely to exacerbate a fixed mindset, making them more reluctant to risk encountering failure in the future. The incremental mindset is the one most likely to lead to success – but a more profound point is that possessing an incremental outlook is a happier way to be, even if it *never* results in any particularly outstanding success. It allows you to abandon the stressful and tiring struggle of perfectionism. It's a win-win proposition, for which the only precondition is a heartfelt willingness to lose.

Interestingly, we may once have been much more willing to think about failure in this way. Prior to the nineteenth century, the historian Scott Sandage has argued, it was rare to hear the word 'failure' applied to an individual. Certain ventures, such as an attempt to run for office or to start a company, might prove to be failures – but the individual behind such an undertaking would be described as having 'made a failure', not as *being* one. To have made a failure could be depressing, no doubt, and even sometimes catastrophic. But it was not an across-the-board condemnation of an entire human life.

To research his fascinating book *Born Losers*, Sandage had to find creative ways around the survivor bias, which ensures that it is usually only tales of success that find their way into historical archives. Cleverly, he had the idea of using begging letters sent to the oil magnate John D. Rockefeller in the late 1800s. Poring over these and other sources solidified Sandage's hunch that the idea that a *person* could be 'a failure' had sprung directly from the growth of entrepreneurial capitalism over this period. One crucial development, he argues, was the emergence of credit rating agencies, whose role was to sit in judgment upon individuals seeking loans from banks, helping the banks determine the risk they would be taking by making the loan. In a society increasingly dominated by business, a bad credit rating could all too easily come to be seen as a verdict condemning a whole person – and it is from the language of credit rating, Sandage notes, that we take several modern idioms for describing someone's moral worth, such as 'good-for-nothing' and 'first-rate'. Failure, he writes, became transformed from a bump in the road of life to the place at which 'the story stops'. From the middle of the nineteenth century onwards, failure started to be thought of 'not merely [as] a cataclysm that adds to the plot of your life, but [as] something that stops your life cold, because you lose a sense of your future'.

Failure, in short, came to be seen as a kind of death. The message of the most radical proponents of the embrace of failure, like Natalie Goldberg, is that it is the exact opposite: the route to a far more vivid, raw, and acutely experienced way of being alive.

Most of the conventionally successful people who champion the benefits of embracing failure are making a much less radical claim than Goldberg's; they are talking about learning to tolerate failure only as a means to their eventual success. A rare exception is J. K. Rowling, the stratospherically successful author of the *Harry Potter* novels, who in 2008 gave a now-famous graduation speech at Harvard University on the subject of failure. Of course, it is impossible to know for sure how Rowling would feel about failure if it hadn't been followed, in her case, by spectacular success. But she conveyed the distinct impression that she would have felt the same about it even if she had remained obscure, poor, and creatively unfulfilled. Her words chime with many of the insights of the Stoics, the Buddhists, and others into the benefits of negativity, and they are worth quoting at length:

I think it fair to say that by any conventional measure, a mere seven years after my graduation day, I had failed on an epic scale. An exceptionally short-lived marriage had imploded, and I was jobless, a lone parent, and as poor as it is possible to be in modern Britain without being homeless. The fears that my parents had had for me, and that I had had for myself, had both come to pass, and by every usual standard, I was the biggest failure I knew. Now, I am not going to stand here and tell you that failure is fun. That period of my life was a dark one, and I had no idea there was going to be what the press has since represented as a fairytale resolution. I had no idea how far the tunnel extended . . . so why do I talk about the benefits of failure?

Simply because failure meant a stripping away of the
inessential. I stopped pretending to myself that I was
anything other than what I was, and began to direct all my
energy into finishing the only work that mattered to me . . .
I was set free, because my greatest fear had been realised,
and I was still alive. [Failure] gave me an inner security that
I had never attained by passing examinations . . . Such
knowledge is a true gift, for all that it is painfully won, and
it has been worth more than any qualification I ever earned.

8

Memento Mori

Death as a Way of Life

If I had my life over I should form the habit of nightly composing myself to thoughts of death. I would practice, as it were, the remembrance of death . . . without an ever-present sense of death, life is insipid. You might as well live on the whites of eggs.

– Inspector Mortimer in Muriel Spark's *Memento Mori*

AT ONE POINT DURING the course of the 200,000-line Indian spiritual epic the *Mahabharata*, the warrior-prince Yudhisthira is being cross-questioned about the meaning of existence by a nature spirit on the banks of a lake, which is the sort of thing that happens in the *Mahabharata* all the time. 'What is the most wondrous thing in the world?', the spirit wants to know. Yudhisthira's reply has become one of the poem's best-known lines: 'The most wondrous thing in the world is that although, every day, innumerable creatures go to the abode of Death, still man thinks that he is immortal.'

'Wondrous' is a good way of putting it. Again and again, we have seen how merely not wanting to think certain thoughts or to feel certain emotions isn't sufficient to eliminate them. That's why nobody ever wins Daniel Wegner's 'white bear challenge', why self-help affirmations often make people feel worse, and why confronting worst-case scenarios is almost always preferable to trying to pretend they couldn't happen. But mortality seems a baffling exception to this rule. Death is everywhere, unavoidable, and uniquely terrifying. Yet as long as it's not impinging on us immediately – through recent bereavement, or a life-threatening illness, or a narrowly survived accident – many of us manage to avoid all thoughts of our own mortality for months, even years, at a time. The more you reflect on this, the stranger it seems. We are perfectly capable of feeling acute self-pity about more minor predicaments, at home or at work, on a daily basis. Yet the biggest predicament of all goes by, for the most part, not consciously worried about. 'At bottom,' wrote Freud – sweepingly, as usual, but in this case persuasively – 'no one believes in his own death.'

This apparent nonchalance in the face of mortality looks stranger still in light of the fact that we *do* talk about death, all the time, yet somehow without ever really talking about it. Who reads those magazine features listing 'a hundred things to do before you die' – places to travel, foods to eat, albums to hear – and pays any real attention to the 'before you die' part? If you did, your reaction might well be a cry of existential despair: 'Why bother, if I'm just going to die in the end anyway?' (And existential despair, needless to say, is not the response a magazine editor usually wishes to evoke among readers.) We're captivated by fictional tales of murder, but the 'murder' in a murder mystery rarely has much to do with the realities of death. Even real deaths in news reports can trigger horror, sympathy, or outrage without once prompting the viewer to reflect that the same basic fate, in a few decades at most, awaits him too. The idea of choosing to

think about our own mortality, in a personal sense, as a matter
of daily conversation, strikes us as hilarious – the joke on which,
for example, much of the humour in Woody Allen's 1975 movie
Love and Death rests:

BORIS: Nothingness. Non-existence. Black emptiness.
SONJA: What did you say?
BORIS: Oh, I was just planning my future.

One of the most persuasive explanations of this psychological
puzzle remains the one put forward in 1973 by Ernest Becker, in
his magnum opus *The Denial of Death*. (Another death-fixated
Woody Allen character, Alvy Singer, uses a copy to woo the titular
heroine of *Annie Hall*.) Becker was born in Massachusetts in 1924;
as a drafted soldier he encountered the worst realities of death
while still a young man, helping to liberate a Nazi concentration
camp by the time he had turned twenty-one. The lack of serious
thought we give to mortality, for Becker, is no accident or over-
sight: it is precisely *because* death is so terrifying and significant,
he argues, that we don't think about it. 'The idea of death, the
fear of it, haunts the human animal like nothing else,' his book
begins. But the consequence is that we dedicate our lives to
suppressing that fear, erecting vast psychological fortifications so
that we can avoid confronting it. Indeed, an enormous proportion
of all human activity, in Becker's view, is 'designed largely to avoid
the fatality of death, to overcome it by denying in some way that
it is the final destiny of man'.

We are able to sustain this denial, he explains, because we possess
both a physical self and a symbolic one. And while it is inevitable
that the physical self will perish, the symbolic self – the one that
exists in our minds – is quite capable of convincing itself that it

is immortal. The evidence of this is all around us; in fact, it's so ubiquitous that you might miss it. In Becker's view, all religions, all political movements and national identities, all business ventures, all charitable activity and all artistic pursuits are nothing but 'immortality projects', desperate efforts to break free of death's gravitational pull. We long to think of ourselves not as mortal humans but as immortal 'heroes'. Society itself is essentially a 'codified hero system' – a structure of customs, traditions and laws that we have designed to help us feel part of something bigger, and longer-lasting, than a mere human life. Thanks to our symbol-making capacities, he writes, 'The single organism can expand into dimensions of worlds and times without moving a physical limb; it can take eternity into itself, even as it gaspingly dies.' From this perspective, it isn't only conventionally religious people who depend on the notion of an afterlife. All normally adjusted people, religious or not, unconsciously do so – and 'every society is thus a "religion", whether it thinks so or not'. For Becker, mental illness is a malfunctioning of the internal death-denial machinery. Depressed people are depressed because they try but repeatedly fail to shield themselves, as others manage to do, from the truth that they are not, in reality, cosmically significant heroes – and that pretty soon they're going to die.

Immortality projects may be the cause of plenty of good things – great architecture, great literature, great acts of philanthropy, great civilisations – but in Becker's view they are simultaneously the cause of the worst things, too. Our urge to think of ourselves as heroes doesn't discriminate: it helps explain why we compete in sports or politics or commerce, but also why we fight wars. War represents the ultimate clashing of rival immortality projects: if my sense of immortality relies on my nation's triumph, and yours upon yours, we'll fight longer and harder than if we were seeking only territory or power. 'Making a killing in business or in the battlefield', writes the philosopher Sam Keen, paraphrasing Becker, 'frequently has less to do with economic need or political reality than with the need for assuring ourselves that we have achieved something of lasting worth . . . [Human conflicts] are life-and-death struggles – my gods against your gods, my immortality project against your immortality project.' In other words, we will fight so hard to preserve our symbolic immortality that we will sacrifice our physical lives. In order to deny death, we will die. Even worse, we will deny that this is what we are doing, until the point at which we can deny it no longer. 'One of the main reasons that it is so easy to march men off to war', Becker observes, bleakly, 'is that deep down, each of them feels sorry for the man next to him who will die. Each protects himself in this fantasy until the shock that he is bleeding.'

If Becker is right, the 'wondrous' fact that we behave as if we're immortal isn't so wondrous after all. You don't *fail* to think about your mortality. Rather, your life is one relentless attempt to avoid doing so – a struggle so elemental that, unlike in the case of the 'white bear challenge', for much of the time you succeed.

A few years after *The Denial of Death* became a bestseller, several experimentally minded psychologists realised that Becker's speculations (and, powerful as they were, they were just speculations) could easily be subjected to a more scientific test. If Becker is correct that we spend our lives fiercely but subconsciously trying to evade thoughts of our own death, it ought to follow that people who are explicitly *reminded* of their mortality – who are, in the language of psychology experiments, 'primed' to think about it – would instinctively fight back, by clinging ever harder to their death-denying beliefs and behaviours. This is the hunch underlying the field known evocatively as 'terror management theory', which over the last two decades has generated numerous persuasive examples of just how deeply the denial of death affects us.

One typical set of terror management experiments, at Rutgers University in New Jersey, in 2003, unfolded as follows. First, the participants were fed a banal cover story about why they had been invited to take part – the study, they were informed, concerned 'the relationship between personality attributes and opinions about social issues'. Mortality wasn't mentioned. Then they were asked to fill out some lengthy and largely mundane questionnaires, which were identical for each participant except when it came to two specific questions. For one set of respondents, those questions were about something mundane, too: their television-watching habits. For the others – described as the 'mortality salience' group – the questions focused on death. One was: 'Please briefly describe the emotions that the thought of your own death arouses in you.' The other question demanded that respondents 'jot down, as specifically as you can, what you think will happen to you as you physically die, and once you are physically dead.'

Then came a second exercise, which was the study's real point. Participants were asked to read a short essay that expressed strong support for the foreign policies of George Bush, then to decide how far they agreed with it. 'Personally,' read the essay, 'I endorse the actions of President Bush and the members of his administration who have taken bold action in Iraq. I appreciate our President's wisdom regarding the need to remove Saddam Hussein from power . . . We need to stand behind our President and not be distracted by citizens who are less than patriotic.'

Again and again, in terror management experiments, people who have been shifted into this condition of 'mortality salience' – prompted to think about death – demonstrate markedly different attitudes from those who haven't. Their responses to questions lend weight to the hypothesis that they are grasping hold of their immortality projects much more firmly than usual, in reaction against being reminded that they will die. Christians show more negativity towards Jews. Moralistic people become more moralistic. Where money is involved, people become less willing to share or to trust, and more eager to hoard whatever wealth they can. And at Rutgers in 2003, when asked how far they shared the views of the essay about President Bush, people in a state of 'mortality salience' were significantly more willing to endorse its author's fighting talk. Other studies have shown a similar preference, in conditions of mortality salience, for authoritarian personalities over 'relationship-oriented' ones. It seems clear that Bush benefited greatly from mortality salience effects in the real world as well. The terrorist attacks on 11 September 2001 would have functioned like an extreme version of the death questions on a terror-management questionnaire, startling anyone who heard the news into the realisation that they, too, could go into the office one ordinary morning and die. 'It is [fear] that makes people so willing to follow brash, strong-looking demagogues with tight jaws and loud voices,' wrote Becker – leaders 'who seem most capable of cleansing the world of the vague, the weak, the uncertain, the evil. Ah, to give oneself over to their direction – what calm, what relief.'

Mortality salience makes itself felt in numerous other, sometimes unexpected ways. Experimental subjects who have been prompted to think about death demonstrate more intense reactions of disgust to discussions of human bodily waste. They agree more strongly with statements such as 'If I see someone vomit, it makes me sick to my stomach.' They are more likely to rank certain hypothetical scenarios as 'very disgusting', for example seeing maggots on a piece of meat. This response, researchers argue, shows that participants are struggling to buffer themselves against confronting reminders of their 'creatureliness' – of the fact that, like other animals, they are physically mortal. 'Disgust', one such paper states, enables 'humans to elevate themselves above other animals and thereby defend against death'. (This reaction to mortality, following Becker's logic, may also help explain some cultures' taboos against menstruating women, and why defecation and urination are generally done in private.) People in a condition of mortality salience, it transpires, are also more likely to be sympathetic to the theory of 'intelligent design', perhaps for similar reasons: if you can convince yourself that life didn't emerge meaninglessly from the primordial swamp, it's easier to feel that it won't end in meaningless extinction, either.

In view of all this, the argument that it could be *beneficial* to live with more daily consciousness of one's mortality might sound impractical at best. For one thing, Becker's argument seems to suggest that the denial of death is far too deep-rooted for us ever to hope to unseat it. Besides, if it is the motivation for all sorts of extraordinary human achievements, would you really even want to do so? Yet since the time of the ancient Greeks, certain radical thinkers have taken the position that a life suffused with an awareness of one's own mortality – as a matter of everyday habit, not just when direct encounters with death force our hand – might be a far richer kind of existence. It is also surely a more authentic one. Death *is* a fact of life, however hard we might try to deny it. In fact, the 'cult of optimism', with its focus on positivity at all costs, can itself be seen as a kind of 'immortality project' – one that promises a future vision of happiness and success so powerful and all-encompassing that it might somehow transcend death. Positive thinkers, it's true, do pay lip-service to mortality awareness, with their homilies about 'living each day as if it were your last'. But this is usually delivered as mere motivational advice, as a spur to get moving, to start realising your greatest ambitions. And if those ambitions are themselves simply more immortality projects, we have not really come any closer to living with an awareness of death.

Ernest Becker's appointment with mortality came tragically early: a year before *The Denial of Death* was published, he was diagnosed with colon cancer, at the age of forty-seven. Two years later, Sam Keen visited him, literally on his deathbed, in a hospital ward in Vancouver one rainy day in February 1974. Keen was there to conduct an interview with Becker for *Psychology Today*. 'Well,' Becker told him, 'now you'll have a chance to see whether I lived as I thought.' He had requested only a minimum of pain-killing medication, he explained, so as to remain 'clear' in his final inter-actions with his family, and in his dying. The denial of death might have structured all human civilisation, but it wasn't the best way, Becker believed, for an individual to deal with his own death. 'Gradually, reluctantly,' Keen wrote later, 'we are beginning to acknowledge that the bitter medicine [Becker] prescribes – contemplation of the horror of our own death – is, paradoxically, the tincture that adds sweetness to mortality.' The interview was published a month after their meeting, in March. A few days afterwards, Becker died.

It may be hard to swallow the idea that we should spend more time contemplating death, but there are some powerful and prag-matic arguments for doing so. Consider, for example, the Stoic technique of the 'premeditation of evils'. Death is going to happen, Seneca would say, and so it must be preferable to be mentally prepared for its approach, instead of shocked into the sudden realisation that it is imminent. In any case, our subconscious strivings not to think about death are never entirely successful: long before your own death becomes a probability, you'll occasionally find yourself in the grip of that middle-of-the-night panic so vividly captured by Philip Larkin in his poem 'Aubade': 'Unresting death, a whole day nearer now . . . Flashes afresh to hold and horrify.' Better, surely, to avoid such horror by normalising the prospect if possible.

But how to go about doing this? The denial of death isn't like most other problems, which weigh on us so heavily that we may eventually be driven to find a way to solve them. The whole problem is that, most of the time, it doesn't feel like a problem at all. Subconsciously assuming that you're immortal makes for a much easier existence, so long as you can keep it up. How, then, to fight this instinct and choose, as a matter of daily living, to confront death instead?

Solving this conundrum sounded like it might be a job for someone who was both a philosopher and a psychotherapist, and so in search of answers I turned to Lauren Tillinghast, a woman whose business cards and website described her as a 'philosophical counsellor'. She was part of a contemporary movement among philosophers who felt that they were returning the discipline to its Socratic roots, as a therapeutic practice intended to soothe the soul, not just an academic exercise in theory-spinning. Tillinghast did her fair share of such theorising; she'd published articles in philosophy journals with titles such as 'What Is an Attributive Adjective?' and 'The Classificatory Sense of "Art"'. But she also had a consulting office, in downtown Manhattan, a bright and neatly furnished room hidden inside an ageing office building that was home to a number of more conventional therapists, psychiatrists, and counsellors. She was in her early forties, and had the practised, friendly neutrality of a woman accustomed to listening non-judgmentally to other people's problems. She poured me some mint tea into a white china cup, ushered me to an armchair, and didn't flinch when I told her I wanted to talk about death – and, specifically, how one might learn to choose to live with greater awareness of one's mortality. 'Well, that's a pretty big topic,' she said. But we had to start somewhere, and we decided to begin with Epicurus.

The first step in trying to become more comfortable with your mortality involves attempting to reduce the terror induced by the mere thought of death. (If you can't manage that, you're unlikely to get much further.) Tillinghast explained that philosophers had often sought to achieve this by means of rational argument: if you can be persuaded that the fear of death is illogical, you're more likely to be able to let go of it. The ancient Greek philosopher Epicurus – a contemporary of Zeno of Citium, the original Stoic – had made one of the earliest attempts. Before him, the philosophical consensus on death, broadly speaking, was that it wasn't really final: the best argument for not being scared of it was that a glorious afterlife might follow. Epicurus's argument is the mirror-image of this. If life *doesn't* continue beyond death, he points out, that's an excellent reason not to be scared of it, either. 'Death is nothing to us,' he says, 'since when we are, death has not come, and when death has come, we are not.' You might fear a painful dying process. You might dread the pain of losing others to death; our focus here is not on the terrible pain of grief. But fearing being dead yourself makes no sense. Death spells the end of the experiencing subject, and thus the end of any capacity for experiencing the state we fear. Or as Einstein put it: 'The fear of death is the most unjustified of all fears, for there's no risk of accident to one who's dead.' The one great fear that governs our lives, from this perspective, stands exposed as a kind of error. It's as if, instead of imagining death, we had all along been imagining something more like being buried alive – deprived of all the benefits of existence, yet somehow still forced to experience the deprivation.

One powerful counterargument to this position is that our fear doesn't come from imagining death *wrongly*, but from the fact that we can't imagine it at all. That was roughly Freud's view of the matter: that what we call 'the fear of death' is really more of a horrified seizing-up in the face of something utterly inconceivable. But as the contemporary philosopher Thomas Nagel points out, there's something wrong with this argument, too – because there's nothing about 'unimaginable' states that is terrifying by definition. We can't imagine what it's like to be in a state of dreamless sleep, either, but we surrender to it every night, and very few of us do so with feelings of terror. 'People who are averse to death', Nagel notes drily, 'are not usually averse to unconsciousness.'

Epicurus has a second, connected point to make about the non-scariness of death, which has become known as the 'argument of symmetry'. Why do you fear the eternal oblivion of death, he wonders, if you don't look back with horror at the eternal oblivion before you were born – which, as far as you were concerned, was just as eternal, and just as much an oblivion? Vladimir Nabokov famously opens his memoir *Speak, Memory* with lines that drive this point home: 'The cradle rocks above an abyss, and common sense tells us that our existence is but a brief crack of light between two eternities of darkness. Although the two are identical twins, man, as a rule, views the prenatal abyss with much more calm than the one he is headed for.' If you weren't traumatised by not having yet been born, it seems logical not to worry about being traumatised by being dead. But of course, Tillinghast pointed out, 'it's not very useful, for most people, to point out that a fear is *illogical*. It doesn't make it go away.'

There's another problem with all these efforts to make *being dead* a less frightening prospect, which is this: who says that being dead is the problem in the first place? When we contemplate our own personal mortality, the real sting is surely that we're going to *stop being alive*, and lose all the benefits we enjoy as a result of living. 'People don't generally come to me because they fear the oblivion of being dead,' Tillinghast said. 'But the idea of everything that makes life *lifely* drawing to a close – well, that's a much greater source of anxiety.' It is true, of course, that you won't be around to *experience* being deprived of those benefits, so fearing that deprivation is arguably unjustifiable. But as Nagel argues, in an essay entitled simply 'Death', the fact that you shouldn't fear death doesn't mean that it isn't a bad thing. By way of analogy, he says, imagine an adult who suffers a severe brain injury and is reduced to the mental state of a three-year-old. He might be perfectly happy in his new condition, but nobody would disagree that something bad had still happened to the adult he once was. It makes no difference that the adult is no longer around. No matter how persuasive you find Epicurus's arguments against *fearing* death, it doesn't follow that death is not *bad*.

This distinction is crucial, because it begins to make sense of the idea that a greater degree of mortality awareness might be part of the recipe for happiness. For as long as you're terrified by the idea of your mortality, you can't really be expected to swallow Ernest Becker's 'bitter medicine' and voluntarily opt to spend more time thinking about your own death. On the other hand, trying to embrace death as a *good* thing would seem to be asking

far too much of yourself. It might not necessarily even be desir-
able, since it could cause you to place less value on being alive.
But coming to understand death as something that there is no
reason to fear, yet which is still bad because of what it brings to
an end, might be the ideal middle path. The argument is a thor-
oughly down-to-earth, pragmatic, and Stoic one: the more that
you remain aware of life's finitude, the more you will cherish it,
and the less likely you will be to fritter it away on distractions.
'Look at it like going to a really nice restaurant,' said Tillinghast.
'You take it as a fact that the meal isn't going to last forever. Never
mind if that's the way it should be, or whether you feel like you're
owed more meal, or you resent the fact that the meal isn't eternal.
It's just the case that you have this one meal. So it would make
sense, wouldn't it, to try to suck the marrow out of it? To focus
on the flavours? To not let yourself be distracted by irritation at
the fact that there's a woman at the next table wearing too much
perfume?' The psychotherapist Irvin Yalom, in his book *Staring
at the Sun*, points out that many of us live with the dim fear that
on our deathbeds we'll come to regret how we spent our lives.
Remembering our mortality moves us closer to the deathbed
mindset from which such a judgment might be made – thus
enabling us to spend our lives in ways that we're much less likely
to come to regret.

Truly to confront your own mortality, Yalom argues, is to
undergo an awakening – a total shift in perspective that fundamentally transforms how it feels to be alive. And it is not necessarily remotely pleasant. He recalls the reflections of one of his
therapy patients, a woman in her early thirties: 'I suppose the
strongest feelings came,' she told him, 'from realising that it would
be *me* who will die – not some other entity, like Old-Lady-Me,
or Terminally-Ill-and-Ready-to-Die me. I suppose I always

thought of death obliquely, as something that *might* happen, rather than that would happen.' To make that switch, Yalom insists, is not merely to ratchet up the intensity with which you live, but to alter your relationship to life. It is a transformation he describes, borrowing the language of the philosopher Martin Heidegger, as a move from focusing on 'how things are' to the fact 'that things are' – on the sheer astonishing *is*-ness of existence.

This is the real distinction between mortality awareness as a way of life, on the one hand, and those clichéd slogans about 'living each day as if it were your last' on the other. The slogans may be motivational – a reminder to get down to the important stuff before it's too late. But Yalom is talking about a transformation that redefines what constitutes the 'important stuff'. When you really face mortality, the ultimate and unavoidable worst-case scenario, everything changes. 'All external expectations, all fear of embarrassment or failure – these things just fall away in the face of death, leaving only what is truly important,' Apple's founder Steve Jobs once said, in a speech that was speedily co-opted by several gurus of positive thinking, though in truth its message struck fatally at the heart of theirs. 'Remembering that you are going to die is the best way that I know to avoid the trap of thinking you have something to lose. You are already naked.'

Start thinking this way, Yalom points out, and it becomes a virtuous circle. Living more meaningfully will reduce your anxiety about the possibility of future regret at not having lived meaningfully – which will, in turn, keep sapping death of its power to induce anxiety. As he puts it, there is a positive correlation between the fear of death and the sense of unlived life. Live a life suffused with the awareness of its own finitude, and you can hope to finish it in something like the fashion that Jean-Paul Sartre hoped to die: 'quietly . . . certain that the last burst of my heart would be inscribed on the last page of my work, and that death would be taking only a dead man'.

After wrestling for a while with the ideas of Becker, Epicurus, Thomas Nagel and Irvin Yalom, I decided to take a trip to Mexico. I had suspected for some time that this would prove necessary if I was really going to understand the role of mortality awareness in daily life. I had often seen it claimed that Mexico had a unique attitude towards death. By common agreement, it was one of the few countries that still had an active tradition of *memento mori* – rituals and customs designed to encourage regular reflections on mortality – and, according to several recent international surveys, it was also one of the happiest; perhaps even the happiest or second happiest nation in the world, in fact, depending on the measures used. The most famous example of this attitude towards death is the annual celebration known as the Day of the Dead, when Mexicans toast those who have died – and death itself – with copious quantities of tequila, and bread in the shape of human remains; people build shrines in their homes, throng city squares, and conduct all-night vigils at the graves of deceased relatives. But this way of thinking runs deeper than a national holiday each November. As the celebrated Mexican essayist Octavio Paz writes, in his book *The Labyrinth of Solitude*: 'The word "death" is not pronounced in New York, in Paris, in London, because it burns the lips . . . the Mexican, in contrast, is familiar with death, jokes about it, caresses it, sleeps with it, celebrates it; it is one of his favorite toys and his most steadfast love.'

This more intimate relationship with mortality was not always so unusual. Such traditions date at least to ancient Rome. There, according to legend, generals who had been victorious in battle would instruct a slave to follow behind as they paraded through the streets; the slave's task was to keep repeating, for the general's benefit, a warning against hubris: *memento mori*, 'remember you shall die'. Much later, in Christian Europe, *memento mori* became a staple of the visual arts: symbols of death appeared frequently in still-life paintings, sometimes including skulls intended to represent those of the artists' patrons. Public clocks featured automata representing death, and sometimes the Latin slogan '*Vulnerant omnes, ultima necat*' as a reminder of the effect of the passing minutes: 'Every [hour] wounds, and the last one kills.' The specific motivation for contemplating mortality differed from era to era, and culture to culture. In the ancient world, it had much to do with remembering to savour life as if it were a delicious meal, as Lauren Tillinghast had advised; for later Christians, it was often more a case of remembering to behave well in anticipation of the final judgment.

I'd been especially intrigued to hear about one contemporary example of death-awareness in Mexican daily life. Santa Muerte was the name of a new religion (according to its followers) or a Satanic cult (in the eyes of the Catholic Church) which worshipped death itself – the figure known as La Santa Muerte, or Saint Death. The movement had sprung up several decades ago in the toughest neighbourhoods of Mexico City, among prostitutes and drug dealers and the very poor – people for whom both the Mexican government and the Catholic Church had failed to provide. Instead, they prayed to Santa Muerte for protection from death, for a gentle death, or sometimes for death to their enemies. Now, as a result of immigration, Santa Muerte had spread to parts of the United States; it was also said that some of Mexico's most powerful businessmen and politicians kept secret death-shrines at home. And although many of the followers of Saint Death

were law-abiding Mexicans – they had marched in the streets
to protest the government's attempts to characterise the movement as nothing but a band of criminals – it was nonetheless
true that it had become the religion of choice of the *narcotra-
ficantes*, the ruthless drug-smuggling gangs of Mexico's north.
At the movement's main shrine in the *barrio* of Tepito in Mexico
City – where a life-sized model of a skeleton, laden with jewel-
lery, stood in a glass case on a side-street – some of the country's most violent men came to leave offerings of dollar bills,
cigarettes, and marijuana. Whatever other significance the
movement had, being a follower of Santa Muerte seemed to
entail devoting oneself to an especially extreme form of *memento
mori* – to organising one's life around the omnipresence of
death. 'In a world of facts,' writes Paz, 'death is merely one
more fact. But since it is such a disagreeable fact, contrary to
all our concepts and to the very meaning of our lives, the
philosophy of progress . . . pretends to make it disappear, like
a magician palming a coin.' In Mexico, Santa Muerte was where
you turned if the circumstances of your life made this sleight-
of-hand impossible – if the constant fear of violent death
removed the option of ignoring your mortality.

I did visit Tepito during my time in Mexico, a few days before
the Day of the Dead itself, though it didn't prove the most
successful of assignments. I had been warned not to get there by
hailing a taxi from the street, because of the risk of kidnapping;
as a reporter, I have no real thirst for danger, and arguably I
shouldn't have gone at all. 'Foreigners for obvious reasons *never*
go to Tepito!', someone advised, in an internet forum that I probably shouldn't have consulted. 'Only idiots and the ignorant visit
Tepito,' warned someone else. A few days earlier, an armed gang
had gunned down six people on a street corner there, in the

middle of the day. In the newspapers, it was reported that the police had written off whole sections of it as too dangerous to bother trying to patrol. A filmmaker based in Mexico City, who'd made a documentary about Tepito, declined to accompany me there, citing safety concerns. And a restaurateur in a smarter part of the city had cheerily passed along what she claimed was a well-known saying: in Tepito, even the rats carried guns. My walk into Tepito was therefore, if nothing else, a pretty good exercise in *memento mori* for myself.

I set off from the heart of the city in the middle of the morning, through shopping streets and Mexico City's business district, then along bigger highways lined with scrappy, busy markets, until the streets grew narrower and the buildings smaller again, and I found myself in Tepito. The core of the neighbourhood was another cacophonous market – Tepito is notorious as a centre for the sale of counterfeit and stolen goods – but in my search for the Santa Muerte shrine I soon left the main roads and plunged into the deserted backstreets, where rats scuttled from towering piles of rubbish. I hurried past darkened doorways, growing nervous.

In the event, the scene at the shrine itself was festive. Around twenty people were waiting in an orderly line to pay their respects to the skeleton, which was resplendent in purple and orange necklaces and a lace shawl. Some carried their own, smaller statuettes, or bottles of spirits to leave as a gift; one or two blew cigar or cigarette smoke over the skeleton when they came to the front of the line, in what I later learned was a rite of spiritual cleansing. The devotees chatted and laughed – men and women, elderly women and muscular young men, some with newborn babies and toddlers in tow.

Having been unable to persuade a translator to come with me to the *barrio*, I was forced to rely on my terrible Spanish to start a conversation with a woman carrying a foot-high Death statue under her arm. Several other people in the line turned to stare.

She didn't want to talk. The atmosphere in my immediate vicinity quickly turned less festive. I was intruding. Besides, it was quite possible that some of those around me wouldn't want to talk to any reporter or any stranger: people came to Santa Muerte, according to the Mexican essayist Homero Aridjis, 'to ask her "protect me tonight because I am going to kidnap or assault somebody"'. It was a struggle to imagine a life in which death played quite so central a role. Then again, the great truth that was underlined by the scene at the shrine – where the generations mingled as they waited in line – was that death was a subject in which everyone had an inescapable interest.

As a pale, skinny Englishman, though, I was prominently out of place. And a muscular man in a black sleeveless vest, who seemed to be standing guard over the shrine, appeared to have noticed this. He glared at me. There was as much amusement as menace in his glare, since it was embarrassingly plain that I posed him no physical threat. Still, he tilted his head in such a way as to indicate the direction in which he believed I should now proceed: away from the shrine and back to the main street.

It was shortly after this that I made the decision to leave Tepito.

I had better luck on the Day of the Dead itself. (Celebrations begin on the last day of October, but the festival reaches its peak on 2 November.) Through a friend of a colleague, I'd made contact with a local retired taxi-driver named Francisco, who spoke decent English and had a sideline as a 'fixer' for journalists visiting Mexico City. At dusk, he pulled up outside my hotel in a severely battered grey van. 'It's a very safe car,' he said, beaming, though I hadn't asked, then added, 'My other car was in an accident – and now my brother cannot use his leg!' I didn't pursue the subject.

Francisco, as he'd explained to me on the phone a few days earlier, knew his way round the tiny settlements in the countryside outside the capital where the Day of the Dead was still *auténtico* – not commercialised or touristic but haunting and pure, and where villagers spent the entire night conducting vigils in local cemeteries, communing with the corpses of their relatives. It wasn't really in my interests to start quibbling about road safety.

In Mexico City, the official municipal celebrations were reaching their peak. The historical central square, the Zócalo, was packed with families strolling among carts selling bone-shaped bread and sugar skulls. People – adults and children – were everywhere dressed as death: boys as hollow-eyed vampires in stiff starched collars, women as 'La Catrina', the iconic Mexican image of death as a woman in a broad-brimmed hat. On many corners, there were altars to the dead, bedecked with papier-mâché skulls. Such traditions stretched back centuries, but they had been integrated into the life of a busy, modern city. In the offices of banks and insurance companies downtown, I'd been told, desks were often turned into altars. It was commonplace for colleagues to write comic poetry to each other, predicting the manner in which they might die.

But Francisco and I were headed away from the bustling squares, onto wide, chaotic highways – dodging stray dogs and suicidally piloted minibuses – and then, as night fell, on empty, unlit country lanes. 'You know,' Francisco said after we had passed another dimly illumined roadside statue of death, looming from the blackness, 'when I was a child, on this day, we would go from house to house, to make a joke about how each person was going to die. So if someone smokes too much, you brought him cigarettes, to make a joke about how he was going to die from too much smoking.' He smiled at the memory. 'Or if there was someone who lived in that house who had died from too much smoking, then you could bring cigarettes as a gift to remember him.'

'Didn't people get offended?'

'Offended?'

'You know. Insulted.'

'No, why?' He turned to look at me. 'I think that this is only in Mexico, though.'

He was largely right about that. Elsewhere in the Catholic world, 2 November is All Souls' Day, designated since the eighth century as an occasion for mournful remembrance of the dead. But when the *conquistadors* reached Mexico, in the fifteenth century, they encountered celebrations of death among the Mayan and Aztec populations far more elaborate than their own: the Aztecs honoured their 'lady of the dead', Mictecacihuatl, with a two-month festival of bonfires, dance and feasting. The colonists were determined to replace all this with something more sombre and more Christian. The Day of the Dead – with its strange mixture of Christianity and pre-Christian religions, mourning and humour – is a testament to the incompleteness of their victory.

There were cultures that took *memento mori* to even greater extremes. The sixteenth-century essayist Michel de Montaigne was fond of praising the ancient Egyptians – 'who in the height of their feasting and mirth, caused a dried skeleton of a man to be brought into the room, to serve as a memento to their guests'. (A writer's working space, Montaigne also believed, ought to have a good view of the cemetery; it tended to sharpen one's thinking.) And in the *Satipatthana Sutta*, one of the formative texts of Buddhism, the Buddha urges his monks to travel to charnel grounds in order to seek out – as objects upon which to meditate – one of the following:

. . . a corpse, one or two days old, swollen up, blue-black in colour, full of corruption; a corpse eaten by crows; a frame-work of bones, flesh hanging from it, bespattered with blood, held together by the sinews; bones, scattered in all directions, bleached and resembling shells; bones heaped together, after the lapse of years, weathered and crumbled to dust . . .

'Corpse practice', as it was known, was intended to lead the medi-tating monk to the realisation that – as the Buddha is supposed to have phrased it – 'This body of mine also has this nature, has this density, cannot escape it.'

Francisco and I drove on. Eventually, after a diversion to a tiny town to eat pork *chilaquiles* from a roadside stall, and to watch a procession of churchgoers bearing framed photographs of dead relatives, we arrived at his intended destination: the village of San Gregorio Atlapulco. It was chilly, and almost midnight. At first all I could see was an orange glow in the black sky; then, rounding a bend in the road, we came suddenly upon its source. The village cemetery was covered in hundreds of candles and blanketed everywhere in marigold petals, sending a soft orange light into the sky.

Francisco parked the van, and we walked into the cemetery. It took a moment for my eyes to adjust to what I was seeing. Many of the gravestones were only rough concrete slabs or stubby pieces of wood, but almost none were unattended. Next to each, sitting in folding chairs or cross-legged on the ground, were groups of two, three, or four people, sometimes more, holding murmured conversations and drinking tequila from paper cups. In one corner, a mariachi band in full costume strolled from grave to grave, serenading every headstone in turn. I stopped a woman who was carrying armfuls of rugs and chairs towards a nearby headstone, and asked what she was doing. 'Oh, it's my mother,' she said brightly, gesturing at the grave. 'We come every year.'

It would be entirely wrong to give the impression that the Day of the Dead – or Mexico's approach to *memento mori* in general, for that matter – represented any kind of shortcut around the inescapable and scarring realities of grief. The participants in the cemetery vigils were not, by and large, those still reeling from the impact of having recently been bereaved. The idea, in any case, was not to adopt a rictus grin in the face of death. That approach is surely the 'cult of optimism at its worst': it doesn't work, and even if it did, it wouldn't be an appropriate response to loss. The Day of the Dead is not an effort to remake something horrifying as something unproblematic; it is, precisely, a rejection of such binary categories. What was happening in the cemetery was *memento mori* at its most powerful – a ritual that neither repressed thoughts of death, nor sought, in the manner of an American or British Hallowe'en, to render it saccharine and harmless. It was about letting death seep back into life.

'In our tradition,' observes the writer Victor Landa, who was raised in Mexico, 'people die three deaths. The first is when our bodies cease to function; when our hearts no longer beat of their own accord, when our gaze no longer has depth or weight, when the space we occupy slowly loses its meaning. The second death comes when the body is lowered into the ground . . . the third death, the most definitive death, is when there is no one left alive to remember us.' Death was omnipresent that night in the cemetery, and yet – precisely as a consequence of that – the third kind of death was absent. An entire town was remembering. And remembering, too, their own mortality, which differed from their dead relatives' only in the sense that it had not claimed them yet.

You need not engage in cemetery vigils to practise *memento mori*, however. You can start much smaller. The psychologist Russ Harris suggests a simple exercise: imagine you are eighty years old – assuming you're not eighty already, that is; if you are, you'll have to pick an older age – and then complete the sentences 'I wish I'd spent more time on . . . ' and 'I wish I'd spent less time on . . . '. This turns out to be a surprisingly effective way to achieve mortality awareness in short order. Things fall into place. It becomes far easier to follow Lauren Tillinghast's advice – to figure out what, specifically, you might do in order to focus on life's flavours, so as to improve your chances of reaching death having lived life as fully and as deeply as possible.

This kind of smaller habit may actually be the most powerful form of *memento mori*. For it is precisely through such mundane and unassuming rituals that we can best hope to enfold an aware-ness of death into the daily rhythms of life, and thus achieve something of Epicurus's calm rationality in the face of mortality. What lingered in my mind for months after Mexico, in any case, was not the loud celebration of death, though I had seen some of that in central Mexico City. Instead, it was the sense I had absorbed, in San Gregorio Atlapulco, of relaxing alongside mortality, of comfortably coexisting with it, of the companionship of life and death.

Before we left the village that night, some time before two in the morning, I noticed an elderly woman sitting alone on a folding chair near one of the cemetery's boundary walls. She was wrapped in a shawl and appeared to be talking softly to a head-stone.

Tentatively, I approached her. Interrupting felt wrong, but she wasn't hostile; smiling, she nodded at the ledge beside the grave, inviting me to sit. So I sat.

The strains of the mariachi band drifted over from the other side of the cemetery. Some families, I noticed, had built small wood fires to keep warm; a few feet away, Francisco clapped his arms around himself in an effort to generate heat. I looked out over the cemetery, strewn with marigolds and crowded with huddled figures. Beyond its edges, no lights illuminated the blackness, but inside, the fires and the hundreds of flickering candles lent the night a kind of cosiness, despite the chill. The musicians carried on playing. Death was in the air, and all was well.

Epilogue

Negative Capability

IN DECEMBER 1817, THE poet John Keats, then twenty-two years old, went to see the annual Christmas pantomime at the Theatre Royal, in London's Drury Lane. Also in attendance was his friend, the critic Charles Wentworth Dilke, and as they strolled home, the two men fell into conversation – about writing, and specifically about the nature of literary genius. Somewhere between the theatre in Soho and his home in Hampstead, Keats was struck by a realisation, which he set down several days later in a letter to his brothers. That letter records what one Keats biographer has called 'a touchstone moment' in the history of literature:

> I had not a dispute but a disquisition, with Dilke on various subjects; several things dove-tailed in my mind, and at once it struck me what quality went to form a Man of Achievement, especially in Literature, and which Shakespeare possessed so enormously: I mean Negative Capability, that is, when a man is capable of being in uncertainties, mysteries, doubts, without any irritable reaching after fact and reason . . .

There is something both awe-inspiring and perhaps faintly irritating about a twenty-two-year-old not only capable of such insights, but capable of having them so casually, on the way home from the pantomime. For Keats, such observations had always come effortlessly and frequently, as in some sense they needed to; three years later, he was dead. He thought so little of 'negative capability', in fact, that he never used the phrase in writing again, thereby generously providing future literary scholars with the opportunity to write entire books dedicated to unpicking what he might have meant.

At this point in our journey along the negative path to happiness, however, the outline of what he was saying ought at least to sound familiar. Sometimes the most valuable of all talents is to be able *not* to seek resolution; to notice the craving for completeness or certainty or comfort, and *not* to feel compelled to follow where it leads. Keats thought this addiction to certainty and completion was Dilke's biggest flaw, and the poet's verdict on his friend neatly encapsulates a theme we've encountered many times already: 'He will never come at a truth so long as he lives,' Keats wrote, 'because he is always trying at it.' It was the trying – the 'irritable reaching' – that was the whole problem.

More loosely defined, 'negative capability' is really just another term for living in accordance with the 'backwards law' – and it might be a good label to describe the chief talent I kept discovering among the people I encountered in the course of researching this book. What they all shared was this same turn of mind, which I came to visualise as a sort of graceful mental dance step: a willingness to adopt an oblique stance towards one's own inner life; to pause and take a step back; to turn to face what others might flee from; and to realise that the shortest apparent route to a positive mood is rarely a sure path to a more profound kind of happiness. The phrase 'negative capability' also helps to clarify a subtle double meaning in the word 'negative'. It refers both to a set of skills that involve 'not-doing', as opposed to doing – a negative kind of capability – as well as to the fact that this skill involves confronting negative (as in 'unpleasant') thoughts, emotions, and situations.

The point here is not that negative capability is always superior to the positive kind. Optimism is wonderful; goals can sometimes be useful; even positive thinking and positive visualisation have their benefits. The problem is that we have developed the habit of chronically overvaluing positivity and the skills of 'doing' in how we think about happiness, and that we chronically under-value negativity and the 'not-doing' skills, such as resting in uncertainty or getting friendly towards failure. To use an old cliché of therapy-speak, we spend too much of our lives seeking 'closure'. Even those of us who mock such clichés are often motivated by a craving to put an end to uncertainty and anxiety, whether by convincing ourselves that the future is bright, or by resigning ourselves despondently to the expectation that it won't be. What we need more of, instead, is what the psychologist Paul Pearsall called 'openture'. Yes, this is an awkward neologism. But its very awkwardness is a reminder of the spirit that it expresses, which includes embracing imperfection and easing up on the search for neat solutions.

The various approaches we have explored here frequently contradict each other on the level of details; sometimes they seem so intrinsically paradoxical as practically to contradict themselves. But in this broader sense, they all embody 'negative capability'. For the Stoics, the realisation that we can often choose not to be distressed by events, even if we can't choose events themselves, is the foundation of tranquility. For the Buddhists, a willingness to observe the 'inner weather' of your thoughts and emotions is the key to understanding that they need not dictate your actions. Each of these is a different way of resisting the 'irritable reaching' after better circumstances or better thoughts and feelings. But negative capability need not involve embracing an ancient philosophical or religious tradition. It is also the skill you're exhibiting when you move forward with a project – or with life – in the absence of sharply defined goals; when you dare to inspect your failures; when you stop trying to eliminate feelings of insecurity; or when you put aside 'motivational' techniques in favour of actually getting things done.

You might choose, of course, to dedicate your life to Stoicism, like Keith Seddon in his wizard's cottage in Watford; you might undergo a completely life-transforming experience in the manner of Eckhart Tolle. But you can also treat these ideas as a toolkit, from which tools can be borrowed as necessary. Anyone can become somewhat Stoic, or a bit more Buddhist, or practise *memento mori* a little more frequently; unlike far too many self-help schemes, which purport to be comprehensive guides to life, the negative path to happiness isn't an all-or-nothing affair. True negative capability entails moderation and balance and refraining from too much effortful struggling – including in the practice of negative capability. 'Proficiency and the results of proficiency', wrote Aldous Huxley, 'come only to those who have learned the paradoxical art of doing and not doing, of combining relaxation with activity, of letting go as a person in order that the immanent and transcendent Unknown Quantity may take hold.'

And the end result of all of this? The chief benefit of 'openture', Paul Pearsall claimed, is not certitude or even calm or comfort as we normally think of them, but rather the 'strange, excited comfort [of] being presented with, and grappling with, the tremendous mysteries life offers'. Ultimately, what defines the 'cult of optimism' and the culture of positive thinking – even in its most mystically tinged, New Age forms – is that it abhors a mystery. It seeks to make things certain, to make happiness permanent and final. And yet this kind of happiness – even if you do manage to achieve it – is shallow and unsatisfying. The greatest benefit of negative capability—the true power of negative thinking—is that it lets the mystery back in.

One of the worst things about being a motivational speaker, or any other kind of advocate for the power of positive thinking, must be the constant pressure to seem upbeat: if anyone ever catches you scowling, or stressed, or feeling sorry for yourself – all very normal occurrences for anybody, of course – it threatens to undermine everything you stand for. Becoming an advocate for the power of negative thinking, as I gradually did, holds no such hazard. Bad moods are permitted. Still, the ultimate purpose of all these adventures in negativity was supposed to be happiness. So you'd be entitled to wonder whether the philosophies and psychological techniques I encountered actually made me any happier – and which of them, after all the travelling and the reporting was over, retained a place in my life. Did the negative path to happiness really work? To answer that question with a simple yes or no, or to offer up a list of ten surefire tips for negative-thinking success, would be to violate the ethos of the thing. 'Openture' surely demands that we resist such tempting certainties. But I can offer an interim status report.

I did not make it a regular habit to humiliate myself on public transport systems in major cities. Nor did I relocate to rural Mexico to live a life infused with death. So far I haven't even been on another silent meditation retreat since my week in Massachusetts. But in numerous smaller ways, a modest degree of negative capability has become my daily practice. Few days now go by without some occasion on which I'll deploy what I have come to think of as the 'Stoic pause' – which is all that it takes to remember that it's my judgment about the infuriating colleague, or the heavy traffic, or the burned food, that is the cause of my distress, not the situation itself. Even five or ten minutes' *vipassana* meditation, meanwhile, which I manage most mornings, is sufficient to feel as if I've applied a squirt of WD-40 to my mental machinery: for the rest of the day, problematic thoughts and emotions slip by with far less friction. Eckhart Tolle's deceptively simple-sounding question – 'Do you have a problem *right now*?' – is a marvellous antidote to low-level stress. And I certainly could never have finished writing this book without Shoma Morita's insight that there's no need to 'get motivated' (or Get Motivated!) before you get on and act. In friendships and in my relationship with my girlfriend, I came to understand more deeply that happiness and vulnerability are often the same thing. And at least once a week, I have reason to call to mind Albert Ellis's distinction between a very bad outcome and an absolutely terrible one. Imagining worst-case scenarios is one of my greatest sources of solace in life, actually. When you really try to answer, rationally and in detail, the question 'What's the worst that could happen?', the answer is sometimes pretty bad. But it is finitely bad, rather than infinitely terrifying, so there is always a chance of coping with it. Or at least I think there is. I'm acutely aware that, during the time I spent exploring this perspective on life, no great tragedies befell me, and my family and friends largely thrived. Like a good Stoic, I tried to stay conscious of that, so as to derive happiness from feeling gratitude for my good fortune.

But for me personally, the real test of these philosophies may lie in the future.

Already, though, I can see that where these techniques ultimately lead is to somewhere beyond 'techniques', to a different definition of happiness itself. The real revelation of the 'negative path' was not so much the path as the destination. Embracing negativity as a technique, in the end, really makes sense only if the happiness you're aiming for is one that can accommodate negative as well as positive emotions. The aforementioned Paul Pearsall, inventor of 'openture', spent a large part of his life waging a lonely battle of which John Keats would surely have approved: to get the concept of 'awe' accepted by the psychological establishment as one of the primary human emotions, alongside such standards as love, joy, anger, fear, and sadness. 'Unlike all the other emotions,' he argued, awe 'is all of our feelings rolled up into one intense one. You can't peg it as just happy, sad, afraid, angry, or hopeful. Instead, it's a matter of experiencing all these feelings and yet, paradoxically, experiencing no clearly identifiable, or at least any easily describable, emotion.' Awe, he writes, 'is like trying to assemble a complex jigsaw puzzle with pieces missing. There's never any closure in an awe-inspired life, only constant acceptance of the mysteries of life. We're never allowed to know when this fantastic voyage might end ... but that's part of the life-disorienting chaos that makes this choice so thrillingly difficult.' Which seems, to me, as good a description as any of a happiness that is worthy of the name. This kind of happiness has nothing to do with the easy superficialities of positive thinking – with the grinning insistence on optimism at all costs, or the demand that success be guaranteed. It involves much more difficulty – and also much more authenticity – than that.

The negative path to happiness, then, is a different kind of path. But it is also a path to a different kind of destination. Or maybe it makes more sense to say that the path is the destination? These things are excruciatingly hard to put into words, and the spirit of negative capability surely dictates that we do not struggle too hard to do so. 'A good traveller has no fixed plans,' says the Chinese sage Lao Tzu, 'and is not intent upon arriving.' There could be no better way to make the journey.

Acknowledgements

WRITING THIS BOOK AFFORDED me many opportunities to test its arguments by confronting uncertainty, anxiety, the prospect of failure, and occasionally blind terror. I am grateful that I didn't have to rely on positive-thinking affirmations to deal with this, but benefited instead from the skills and time of some extraordinary people. I thank above all my remarkably Stoical editors, Nick Davies at Canongate and Mitzi Angel at Faber and Faber, whose talents vastly improved the text. Among many to whom I'm grateful at Canongate and FSG are Jamie Byng, Cate Cannon, Jaz Lacey-Campbell, Norah Perkins, Octavia Reeve, Angela Robertson and Jeff Seroy.

To say that I am indebted to my agent, Claire Conrad, and to her colleague Tina Bennett in New York, would be a comical understatement; their guidance and encouragement has been indispensable. Thanks to everyone at Janklow & Nesbit.

As well as all the named interviewees, I thank the following people for advice, contacts, comments on chapters, or places to write: Cyntia Barrera, Tor Butler-Cole, Jeremy Chatzky, Clar Ni Chonghaile, Catherine Crawford, Joanna Ebenstein, Kenneth Folk, Jeffy Gibbins, Julia Greenberg, Debbie Joffe-Ellis, Solana Larsen,

Jeff Mikkelson, Mac Montandon, Salvador Oguín and Joanna Tuckman. At a particularly nerve-wracking point in the process of writing this book, I was hugely fortunate to join the community at Brooklyn Creative League, without which I might never have completed it. At *The Guardian,* for assistance or forbearance in differing measures, I thank Emma Cook, Janine Gibson, Clare Margetson, Emily Wilson and Becky Gardiner. Ian Katz doesn't really do forbearance, but I'm grateful to him for much else.

Since this book grew initially from the topics explored in my column for *Guardian Weekend* magazine, its ultimate source, as with so many ideas, is the mind of Merope Mills, the magazine's editor. Others deserving of much thanks include Esther Addley, Anne Bernstein and my friends from York, of whom I'll unfairly single out here Adam Ormond, Rurik Bradbury, Abigail Gibson, Daniel Weyman, Sally Weyman, Rachael Burnett and Robin Parmiter. Emma Brockes continued her indispensable service as outboard brain, and was much more help than any motivational seminar.

I'm by no means sure that it was a wise happiness strategy on the part of Heather Chaplin to decide to embrace this project as wholeheartedly as she did, but it made an incalculable difference. For this and many other reasons I am ridiculously lucky to know her.

Notes

Some of the interviews in this book were originally conducted in the course of reporting assignments for *The Guardian*. In a small number of other cases, scenes have been compressed or dialogue reconstructed from memory.

1: On Trying Too Hard to Be Happy

3   *has been accused of denying access to reporters . . . Lowe denies the charge:* See Eric Anderson, 'Media Barred from Get Motivated! Seminar, at Least for Now', Albany *Times Union* blog 'The Buzz', 21 July 2009; and Tamara Lowe's comment, at blog.timesunion.com/business/media-barred-from -get-motivated-seminar-at-least-for-now/

5   *has filed for bankruptcy:* See Rebecca Cathcart, 'Crystal Cathedral Files for Bankruptcy', *New York Times*, 18 October 2010.

5   *increased economic growth does not necessarily make for happier societies:* This is an endlessly contested subject, with rival psychologists and economists constantly doing battle, and as ever it rests on contentious definitions of happiness. But one of the very biggest and most up-to-date reviews of the data, which found an absence of correlation in the long term between economic growth and improved wellbeing, is Richard Easterlin et al., 'The Happiness–Income Paradox Revisited', *Proceedings of the National Academy of Sciences* 107 (2010): 22463–8.

5   *increased personal income . . . doesn't make for happier people:* See previous note; and see also Daniel Kahneman et al., 'Would You Be Happier If You Were Richer? A Focusing Illusion', *Science* 312 (2006): 1908–10. And perhaps more to the point, it certainly seems to be the case that if you *set out* to

achieve material goals, you'll be less happy than those with other priorities: see Carol Nickerson et al., 'Zeroing in on the Dark Side of the American Dream', *Psychological Science* 14 (2003): 531–6.

5   *Nor does better education:* See for example Robert Witter et al., 'Education and Subjective Well-Being: A Meta-Analysis', *Educational Evaluation and Policy Analysis* 6 (1984): 165–73.

5   *Nor does an increased choice of consumer products:* The canonical resource on this is Barry Schwartz, *The Paradox of Choice* (New York: Ecco, 2003).

5   *Nor do bigger and fancier homes:* Robert H. Frank, 'How Not to Buy Happiness', *Daedalus* 133 (2004): 69–79.

5   *research strongly suggests they aren't usually much help:* One example is Gerald Haeffel, 'When Self-Help Is No Help: Traditional Cognitive Skills Training Does Not Prevent Depressive Symptoms in People Who Ruminate', *Behaviour Research and Therapy* 48 (2010): 152–7. To be fair, studies have shown some specific self-help books to have a beneficial effect, notably *Feeling Good* by David Burns – see Eric Stice et al., 'Randomized Trial of a Brief Depression Prevention Program: An Elusive Search for a Psychosocial Placebo Control Condition', *Behaviour Research and Therapy* 45 (2007): 863–76.

5   *the 'eighteen-month rule':* For more on this, see Steve Salerno, *Sham: How the Self-Help Movement Made America Helpless* (New York: Crown, 2005).

6   *venting your anger doesn't get rid of it:* Brad Bushman, 'Does Venting Anger Feed or Extinguish the Flame? Catharsis, Rumination, Distraction, Anger, and Aggressive Responding', *Personality and Social Psychology Bulletin* 28 (2002): 724–31.

9   *'when you try to stay on the surface of the water . . .':* Both quotations from Alan Watts, *The Wisdom of Insecurity* (New York: Vintage, 1951), 9.

9   *'the harder we try . . .':* Aldous Huxley, *Complete Essays 1939–1956* (Lanham, Maryland: Ivan R. Dee, 2002), 225.

9   *the 'cult of optimism', as the philosopher Peter Vernezze calls it:* Peter Vernezze, *Don't Worry, Be Stoic* (Lanham, Maryland: University Press of America, 2005): xx.

13 *one typical transcript:* Daniel Wegner, *White Bears and Other Unwanted Thoughts* (New York: Guilford Press, 1989), 3.

13 *he explained in one paper:* Daniel Wegner, 'How to Think, Say or Do Precisely the Worst Thing for Any Occasion', *Science* 325 (2009): 48.

14 *'Metacognition . . . occurs when thought takes itself as an object':* Wegner, *White Bears and Other Unwanted Thoughts*, 44.

14 *'Metathoughts are instructions . . .':* Ibid., 54.

15   *when experimental subjects are told of an unhappy event:* Ibid., 128–9; see
      also Daniel Wegner et al., 'Ironic Processes in the Mental Control of
      Mood and Mood-Related Thought', *Journal of Personality and Social
      Psychology* 65 (1993): 1093–1104.

15   *patients who were suffering from panic disorders:* Chris Adler et al.,
      'Relaxation-Induced Panic (RIP): When Resting Isn't Peaceful', *Integrative
      Psychiatry* 5 (1987): 94–100.

15   *Bereaved people who make the most effort to avoid feeling grief:* Wegner,
      White Bears and Other Unwanted Thoughts, 9, in reference to Erich
      Lindemann, 'Symptomatology and Management of Acute Grief', *American
      Journal of Psychiatry* 101 (1944): 141–8.

15   *people instructed not to think about sex:* Wegner, *White Bears and Other
      Unwanted Thoughts*, 149, in reference to Barclay Martin, 'Expression and
      Inhibition of Sex Motive Arousal in College Males', *Journal of Abnormal
      and Social Psychology* 68 (1964): 307–12.

16   *An additional twist was revealed in 2009:* Joanne Wood et al., 'Positive Self-
      Statements: Power for Some, Peril for Others', *Psychological Science* 20
      (2009): 860–6.

19   *'To the extent that positive thinking had become a business in itself':* Barbara
      Ehrenreich, *Bright-Sided* (New York: Metropolitan, 2009), 12.

21   *'There are lots of ways of being miserable':* Edith Wharton, 'The Last
      Asset', in *The Collected Stories of Edith Wharton* (New York: Carroll & Graf,
      2003), 65.

22   *'doing the presumably sensible thing is counterproductive':* Steven Hayes,
      'Hello Darkness: Discovering Our Values by Confronting Our Fears',
      Psychotherapy Networker 31 (2007): 46–52.

2: What Would Seneca Do?

25   *a speech he gave to executives of the investment bank Merrill Lynch:* See Jeanne
      Pugh, 'The Eternal Optimist', *St. Petersburg Times*, 8 June 1985.

26   *Healthy and happy people . . . generally have a less accurate, overly optimistic
      grasp:* The classic study on 'depressive realism' is Lauren Alloy and Lyn
      Abramson, 'Judgment of Contingency in Depressed and Nondepressed
      Students: Sadder but Wiser?', *Journal of Experimental Psychology* 108 (1979):
      441–85.

27   *a particularly high-achieving week at work:* Heather Barry Kappes and
      Gabriele Oettingen, 'Positive Fantasies about Idealized Futures Sap Energies',
      Journal of Experimental and Social Psychology 47 (2011): 719–29.

27   *Oettingen had some of the participants rendered mildly dehydrated:* Ibid.

29   *writes the scholar of Stoicism William Irvine*: In *A Guide to the Good Life: The Ancient Art of Stoic Joy* (New York: Oxford, 2008), Kindle edition.

30   *'Things do not touch the soul'*: Marcus Aurelius, *The Meditations*, Book IV, Trans. George Long; electronic text available at classics.mit.edu/Antoninus /meditations.html

32   *'the single most valuable technique'*: In William Irvine, *A Guide to the Good Life*.

33   *'Whenever you grow attached to something'*: Quoted in William Stephens, 'Epictetus on How the Stoic Sage Loves', at puffin.creighton.edu/phil /Stephens/OSAP%20Epictetus%20on%20Stoic%20Love.htm

35   *'Set aside a certain number of days'*: *Moral Epistles to Lucilius*, Trans. Richard Gummere (Cambridge: Harvard University Press, 1917), 119.

38   *'Constantly regard the universe as one living being'*: Marcus Aurelius, *Meditations*, Book IV.

40   *'Never have I trusted Fortune'*: Seneca, *The Consolation of Helvia*, Trans. Moses Hadas (New York: Norton, 1968), 111–12.

41   *'Do not despise death'*: Marcus Aurelius, *Meditations*, Book IX.

42   *'The cucumber is bitter? Put it down'*: Marcus Aurelius, *Meditations*, Book VIII; the translation here is by Arthur Loat Farquharson (Oxford: Clarendon, 1944).

44   *America's psychologists had voted him the second most influential*: See Michael Kaufman, 'Albert Ellis, Influential Figure in Modern Psychology, Dies at 93', *New York Times*, 24 July 2007.

45   *'Whereupon thirty got up and walked away'*: Myrtle Heery, 'An Interview with Albert Ellis', www.psychotherapy.net/interview/Albert_Ellis

46   *'Nobody took out a stiletto'*: Ibid.

47   *'because . . . when you insist that an undesirable event is awful'*: Albert Ellis, *How to Make Yourself Happy and Remarkably Less Disturbable* (Atascadero, California: Impact, 1999), 60.

3: The Storm Before the Calm

51   *immediately collapse onto the ground*: This anecdote comes from Rick Fields, *How the Swans Came to the Lake: A Narrative History of Buddhism in America* (Boston: Shambhala, 1992), 252.

52   *'Fall, hands a-clasped'*: See Jack Kerouac, *Pomes All Sizes* (San Francisco: City Lights, 1992), 96.

52   *one Kerouac biographer*: Ann Charters, *Kerouac: A Biography* (New York: Macmillan, 1994), 219.

62   *'One realises . . . that one's brain is constantly chattering'*: J. Krishnamurti,

'Dialogue at Los Alamos', March 1984; available at www.jkrishnamurti.org
/krishnamurti-teachings/print.php?tid=1588&chid=1285

64 *a series of experiments conducted in 2009*: For details, and for Fadel Zeidan's
comments, see University of North Carolina at Charlotte release, 'Brief
Training in Meditation May Help Manage Pain, Study Shows', at www
.sciencedaily.com/releases/2009/11/091110065909.htm, and Fadel Zeidan et
al., 'The Effects of Brief Mindfulness Meditation Training on Experimentally
Induced Pain', *The Journal of Pain* 11 (2010): 199–209.

65 *In a related experiment by Zeidan's team:* See Fadel Zeidan et al., 'Brain
Mechanisms Supporting the Modulation of Pain by Mindfulness Meditation',
Journal of Neuroscience 31 (2011): 5540–8.

67 *'If we get the right emotion':* From a talk at the TED conference by Tony
Robbins, viewable online at www.ted.com/talks/tony_robbins_asks_why
_we_do_what_we_do.html

68 *The author Julie Fast:* See Julie Fast, *Get It Done When You're Depressed*
(New York: Alpha Books, 2008).

69 *'Inspiration is for amateurs':* Quoted in Julie Burstein and Kurt Andersen,
Spark: How Creativity Works (New York: HarperCollins, 2011), 13.

70 *'People . . . think that they should':* Shoma Morita, *Morita Therapy and the
True Nature of Anxiety-Based Disorders*, Trans. Akihisa Kondo (Albany:
State University of New York Press, 1998), 53.

70 *'Many western therapeutic methods focus':* See James Hill, 'Morita Therapy',
at www.moritaschool.com/content/morita-therapy.

73 *'Clear mind is like the full moon in the sky':* Stephen Mitchell, Ed., *Dropping
Ashes on the Buddha: The Teaching of Zen Master Seung Sahn* (New York:
Grove, 1994), 51–2.

4: Goal Crazy

75 *In 1996, a twenty-eight-year-old from Indiana:* My account of Christopher
Kayes's travels, his account of the 1996 Everest disaster, and his interpreta-
tion of the 1963 Everest study, along with quotes from Ed Viesturs, James
Lester, Beck Weathers and others are drawn from an interview with Kayes
and from his fascinating book *Destructive Goal Pursuit: The Mount Everest
Disaster* (New York: Palgrave Macmillan, 2006).

80 *a largely forgotten psychology study:* My primary source is Christopher
Kayes, *Destructive Goal Pursuit*, but the study in question is detailed in
James Leste, 'Wrestling with the Self on Mount Everest', *Journal of
Humanistic Psychology* 23 (1983): 31–41.

84 *a journalist from the technology magazine* Fast Company: Lawrence Tabak,

'If Your Goal Is Success, Don't Consult These Gurus', *Fast Company*, 18 December 2007.

85 *'Consider any individual at any period of his life'*: Alexis de Tocqueville, *Democracy in America*, Vol. 2, Trans. George Lawrence (New York: HarperCollins, 2007), 369.

86 *The psychologist Dorothy Rowe argues:* In Tim Lott, 'Why Uncertainty Is Good for You', *The Sunday Times*, 24 May 2009.

87 *Here are the words of one blogger:* See David Cain, 'How to Get Comfortable Not Knowing', at www.raptitude.com/2009/06/how-to-get-comfortable-not-knowing

87 *the economist Colin Camerer and three of his colleagues:* Colin Camerer et al., 'Labor Supply of New York City Cabdrivers: One Day at a Time', *Quarterly Journal of Economics* 112 (1997): 407–41.

89 *a 2009 paper with a heavy-handed pun for its title:* Lisa Ordóñez et al., 'Goals Gone Wild: The Systematic Side Effects of Over-Prescribing Goal Setting', *Academy of Management Perspectives* 23 (2009): 6–16.

90 *One illuminating example of the problem:* My account of GM's 'twenty-nine' campaign is drawn from Sean Cole, 'It's Not Always Good to Create Goals', from the website of the American Public Media radio show Marketplace, accessible at www.marketplace.org/topics/life/its-not-always-good-create -goals, and Drake Bennett, 'Ready, Aim . . . Fail', *Boston Globe*, 15 March 2009.

91 *Edwin Locke and Gary Latham's response:* Edwin Locke and Gary Latham, 'Has Goal Setting Gone Wild, or Have Its Attackers Abandoned Good Scholarship?', *Academy of Management Perspectives* 23 (2009): 17–23.

93 *'When we try to pick out any thing by itself'*: John Muir, *My First Summer in the Sierra* (New York: Houghton Mifflin, 1911), 211.

93 *'The continued existence of complex interactive systems'*: Gregory Bateson, *Steps to an Ecology of Mind* (Chicago: University of Chicago Press, 1972), 124.

94 *'I'm not sure if my goals drove me'*: Steve Shapiro, *Goal-Free Living* (Hoboken, New Jersey: Wiley, 2006), xii.

95 *In survey research he commissioned:* Steve Shapiro, *Goal-Free Living*, v.

96 *A few years ago, the researcher Saras Sarasvathy:* Information and quotations about effectuation come primarily from Leigh Buchanan, 'How Great Entrepreneurs Think', *Inc. Magazine*, February 2011; and the website www .effectuation.org.

99 *'The quest for certainty blocks the search for meaning'*: Erich Fromm, *Man for Himself* (New York: Macmillan, 1947), 45.

99 *'To be a good human'*: In Bill Moyers, *A World of Ideas* (New York: Doubleday, 1989), 448.

5: Who's There?

102 *'a slow movement at first'*: All quotations from Eckhart Tolle are drawn either
from my meeting with him or from his books *The Power of Now* and *A
New Earth*. See Oliver Burkeman, 'The Bedsit Epiphany', *Guardian*, 11
April 2009; Eckhart Tolle, *The Power of Now* (Novato, California: New World
Library, 1999) and *A New Earth* (New York: Dutton, 2005).

105 *'supremely powerful and cunning'*: This and following quotes are from René
Descartes, *Meditations on First Philosophy*, Trans. Michael Moriarty (Oxford:
Oxford University Press, 2008), 16.

106 *'A viewer of* The Matrix': Christopher Grau, Ed., *Philosophers Explore
the Matrix* (New York: Oxford University Press, 2005), 13.

108 *'For my part, when I enter most intimately'*: David Hume, *An Enquiry
Concerning Human Understanding and Selections from a Treatise of Human
Nature*, Ed. Thom Chittom (New York: Barnes and Noble, 2004), 200.

108 *no 'centre in the brain'*: Quoted in Julian Baggini, 'The Blurred Reality of
Humanity', *Independent*, 21 March 2011.

109 *As the psychologist Michael Gazzaniga has demonstrated*: See Michael
Gazzaniga, *The Ethical Brain* (New York: HarperCollins, 2006), 149.

117 *claims Paul Hauck*: Paul Hauck, *Overcoming the Rating Game: Beyond Self-
Love, Beyond Self-Esteem* (Louisville, Kentucky: Westminster John Knox
Press, 1992), 46.

118 *adapted here from the work of . . . Alan Watts*: All quotations from Alan
Watts, *The Wisdom of Insecurity* (New York: Vintage, 1951).

6: The Safety Catch

127 *'a pretty effective spear'*: All quotations from Bruce Schneier come from my
interview with him and from his essay 'The Psychology of Security'. See
Oliver Burkeman, 'Heads in the Clouds', *Guardian*, 1 December 2007; and
Bruce Schneier, 'The Psychology of Security', accessible at www.schneier
.com/essay-155.html

130 *the 2020 Project . . . published a report*: See www.dni.gov/nic/NIC_global
trend2020_s4.html

130 *'the feeling that we live in a time of unusual insecurity'*: Alan Watts, *The
Wisdom of Insecurity* (New York: Vintage, 1951), 14.

131 *'As a matter of fact'*: Ibid., 15.

134 *'To be vulnerable . . . is to be without defensive armour'*: Quoted in Susan
Schwartz Senstad, 'The Wisdom of Vulnerability'; available at voicedialogue
.org/articles-b/Wisdom_Of_Vulnerability.pdf

134 *'You can't selectively numb emotion'*: From a talk at the TED conference by Brené Brown, viewable online at www.ted.com/talks/brene_brown_on _vulnerability.html

135 *'To love at all is to be vulnerable'*: Quoted in Vincent Genovesi, *In Pursuit of Love: Catholic Morality and Human Sexuality* (Collegeville, Minneapolis: Liturgical Press, 1996), 28.

135 *'The truth that many people never understand'*: Thomas Merton, *The Seven Storey Mountain* (New York: Harcourt, 1948), 91.

135 *'Becoming a Buddhist'*: Quoted in Helen Tworkov, 'No Right, No Wrong: An Interview with Pema Chödrön', *Tricycle*, Fall 1993.

136 *'Things are not permanent'*: Ibid.

140 *'It's clear that poverty has crippled Kibera'*: From Jean-Pierre Larroque, 'Of Crime and Camels', blog post at mediaforsocialchange.org/blog/of-crime -and-camels/ 22 July 2001

140 *'I find it so inspiring when you see people'*: See 'Colleen "Inspired" by Poor People', unbylined article at www.metro.co.uk/showbiz/22368-coleen -inspired-by-poor-people

141 *International surveys of happiness*: All World Values Survey data is accessible at www.worldvaluessurvey.org. Also see, for example, 'Nigeria Tops Happiness Survey', unbylined BBC News article, 2 October 2003, at news .bbc.co.uk/2/hi/3157570.stm

141 *Survey data from the Afrobarometer project*: A good overview of this research is Carol Graham and Matthew Hoover, 'Poverty and Optimism in Africa: Adaptation or Survival?', prepared for the Gallup Positive Psychology Summit, October 2006, accessible at www.brookings.edu/views/papers /graham/20061005ppt.pdf

141 *According to mental health researchers*: The study is by the World Health Organization World Mental Health Survey Consortium, entitled 'Prevalence, Severity, and Unmet Need for Treatment of Mental Disorders in the World Health Organization World Mental Health Surveys', and was reported in 'Global Study Finds Mental Illness Widespread', unbylined Associated Press report, 7 July 2004.

145 *'It is simply self-evident'*: Alan Watts, *The Wisdom of Insecurity*, 16.

7: The Museum of Failure

155 *As the journalist Neil Steinberg has noted*: Neil Steinberg, *Complete and Utter Failure* (New York: Doubleday, 1994), 31.

159 *'top 50 per cent of safe drivers'*: Ola Svenson, 'Are We All Less Risky and More Skillful Than Our Fellow Drivers?', *Acta Psychologica* 47 (1981): 143–8.

159 *A fascinating series of studies of working scientists:* See, for example, Kevin
Dunbar, 'Scientific Creativity' from *The Encyclopedia of Creativity*, Ed.
Steven Pritzker and Mark Runco (Waltham, Massachusetts: Academic
Press, 1999): 1379–84; available at www.utsc.utoronto.ca/~dunbarlab
/pubpdfs/DunbarCreativityEncyc99.pdf

160 *'If you're a scientist and you're doing an experiment':* From a PopTech
conference talk by Kevin Dunbar, 'Kevin Dunbar on Unexpected Science',
accessible online at poptech.org/popcasts/kevin_dunbar_on_unexpected
_science

160 *As he explained in an interview with* Wired: See Jonah Lehrer, 'Accept Defeat:
The Neuroscience of Screwing Up', *Wired*, January 2010.

163 *'Think about it':* All quotations from Jerker Denrell are from my interview
with him or from Jerker Denrell, 'Vicarious Learning, Undersampling of Failure,
and the Myths of Management', *Organization Science* 2003 (14): 227–43; and
Jerker Denrell, 'Selection Bias and the Perils of Benchmarking', *Harvard Business
Review*, April 2005.

166 *research into media commentators who make predictions:* Jerker Denrell and
Christina Fang, 'Predicting the Next Big Thing: Success as a Signal of Poor
Judgment', *Management Science* 56 (2010): 1653–67; see also Joe Keohane,
'That Guy Who Called the Big One? Don't Listen to Him', *Boston Globe*, 9
January 2011.

170 *'The dome has a clear brand':* Ros Coward, 'Wonderful, Foolish Dome',
Guardian, 12 March 2001.

171 *'Musing over failure is not a particularly American activity':* Neil Steinberg,
Complete and Utter Failure, 3.

173 *'Downfall . . . brings us to the ground':* Natalie Goldberg, *The Great Failure*
(New York: HarperCollins, 2005), 1–2.

8: Memento Mori

180 *"At bottom . . . no one believes':* Sigmund Freud, *Reflections on War and
Death* (New York: Moffat Yard, 1918), Google Books digitised version, 41.

183 *'Making a killing in business':* Sam Keen, Foreword to Ernest Becker, *The
Denial of Death* (New York: Free Press, 1973), Kindle edition.

184 *One typical set of terror management experiments:* The Rutgers experiments
are Mark Landau et al., 'Deliver Us from Evil: The Effects of Mortality
Salience and Reminders of 9/11 on Support for President George W. Bush',
Personal and Social Psychology Bulletin 30 (2004): 1136–50.

185 *Christians show more negativity towards Jews:* Jeff Greenberg et al., 'Evidence
for Terror Management Theory II: The Effect of Mortality Salience on

Reactions to Those Who Threaten or Bolster the Cultural Worldview', *Journal of Personality and Social Psychology* 58 (1990): 308–18.

185 *Moralistic people become more moralistic:* Abram Rosenblatt et al., 'Evidence for Terror Management Theory: I. The Effects of Mortality Salience on Reactions to Those Who Violate or Uphold Cultural Values', *Journal of Personality and Social Psychology* 57 (1989): 681–90.

185 *more intense reactions of disgust:* Jamie Goldenberg et al., 'I Am *Not* an Animal: Mortality Salience, Disgust, and the Denial of Human Creatureliness', *Journal of Experimental Psychology* 130 (2001): 427–35.

186 *one such paper states:* Ibid.

186 *sympathetic to the theory of 'intelligent design':* Jessica Tracy et al., 'Death and Science: The Existential Underpinnings of Belief in Intelligent Design and Discomfort with Evolution', *PLoS One* 6 (2011): e17349.

187 *'Well,' Becker told him:* See Sam Keen, 'How a Philosopher Dies'; available online at samkeen.com/interviews-by-sam/interviews-by-sam/earnest -becker-how-a-philosopher-dies/

187 *'Gradually, reluctantly':* Sam Keen, Foreword to Ernest Becker, *The Denial of Death.*

190 *as the contemporary philosopher Thomas Nagel points out:* All Nagel quotations are from 'Death' in *Mortal Questions* (New York: Cambridge University Press, 1979), 1–10.

193 *Jean-Paul Sartre:* Quoted in Irvin Yalom, *Staring at the Sun* (San Francisco: Jossey-Bass, 2008), Kindle edition.

194 *also one of the happiest:* Two examples are an Ipsos Global survey that put Mexico third, detailed in 'World Is Happier Place Than in 2007 – Poll', unbylined report, Reuters, 10 February 2012; and the 2010 findings of the Happiness Barometer project, sponsored by the Coca-Cola Company in association with Complutense University of Madrid, which put Mexico in first place: see www.thecoca-colacompany.com/presscenter/happiness_barometer.pdf

198 *'to ask her to "protect me tonight . . ."':* Quoted in Elizabeth Fullerton, 'Booming Death Cult Draws Mexican Gangsters, Police', Reuters, 13 May 2004.

202 *'In our tradition':* Quoted in Judy King, 'Los Dias de los Muertos', in *Mexico Connect*, accessible at www.mexconnect.com/articles/1427-los-dias-de-los -muertos-the-days-of-the-dead

Epilogue: Negative Capability

205 *'a touchstone moment':* Steven Edward Jones, *Satire and Romanticism* (New York: Palgrave Macmillan, 2000), 196.

205 *'I had not a dispute but a disquisition':* Quoted ibid., 195–6.

206 *'He will never come at a truth'*: Quoted in Jacob Wigod, 'Negative Capability and Wise Passiveness', *PMLA* 67 (1952): 383–90.

207 *'openture'*: All Paul Pearsall quotations are from *Awe: The Delights and Dangers of Our Eleventh Emotion* (Deerfield Beach, Florida: Health Communications, 2007).

208 *'Proficiency and the results of proficiency'* Aldous Huxley, *Complete Essays 1939–1956* (Lanham, Maryland: Ivan R. Dec, 2002), 225.

212 *'A good traveller has no fixed plans'*: Lao-tzu, *Tao Te Ching: A New English Version*, translated by Stephen Mitchell (New York: HarperPerennial, 1991), 27.

Index

irritations 66
Irvine, William 29, 32
isolation 146–8

Jobs, Steve 193
judgments 45, 210
    distress and 112–13
    irrational 34, 43, 129
    non-judgmental observation
    64, 65, 72, 74

'kakorrhaphiophobia' 159
Kayes, Christopher 75–82, 86,
    92–3, 95, 97–8, 173
Keats, John 205–6, 211
Keen, Sam 183, 187
Keller, Helen 144
Kerouac, Jack 52
Kibera 136–44
Krakauer, Jon 76
Krishnamurti, Jiddu 62

Labyrinth of Solitude, The (Paz)
    194
Landa, Victor 202
Lao-tzu 212
Larkin, Philip 188
Larroque, Jean-Pierre 140,
    142
Latham, Gary 89–91, 97
'law of attraction' 25
'the law of reversed effort' 8
law of unintended
    consequences 92–3
Lester, James 80–1, 86
Letters from a Stoic (Seneca the
    Younger) 45

Lewis, C. S. 134–5
Lichtenberg, Georg 107
Lives and Opinions of Eminent
    Philosophers (Diogenes
    Laertius) 28
Locke, Edwin 89–91, 97
Long, A. A. 31
Love and Death (movie) 181
Lowe, Tamara 3

McGee, Micki 20
McLoughlin, Coleen 140
McMath, Robert 154–5, 156–7,
    159, 161–2
Magid, Barry 54–8, 64
Mahabharata 179
Marcus Aurelius 28, 30, 38, 41–2
Matrix, The (movie) 106
Mayans 200
meditation 51–5, 57–8, 58–67,
    70–1
Meditation: Now or Never
    (Hagen) 62
Memento Mori (Spark) 179
memento mori tradition 8,
    195–7, 200, 202–3, 208
Menear, Elwood 125–6
Mental Control Laboratory
    (Harvard University) 12
mental health 141
Merton, Thomas 135
Merrill Lynch 25–6
metacognition 14–15
Mexico 10, 194–204
Mictecacihuatl (lady of the
    dead) 200
Mill, John Stuart 7

When Things Fall Apart (Chödrön) 136
white bear challenge 12–13, 180, 183
Why Most Things Fail (Ormerod) 158
Wilson, Paul 52
Winfrey, Oprah 103, 110
Wisdom of Insecurity, The (Watts) 145
Wood, Joanne 16–17
World Values Survey 141
worst-case scenarios 23–50, 180, 210
  Albert Ellis 24, 43–50
  Dr Keith Seddon 36–43
  positive visualisation 25–7, 207
  subway station exercise 23–5, 35, 47, 49–50, 112
  see also Stoicism

Yale Study of Goals 83–5
Yalom, Irvin 192–3, 194
yin and yang 121

Zeidan, Fadel 64–5
Zeno of Citium 27–8, 189
Ziglar, Zig 84